Signs of Fertility

SIGNS OF FERTILITY

The Personal Science
of
Natural Birth Control

By Margaret Nofziger

Illustrations by Jeanne Kahan

MND Publishing, Inc.
Nashville, Tennessee

Published by:

MND Publishing, Inc.
P.O. Box 210813
Nashville, TN 37221

Copyright © 1988 by MND Publishing, Inc.

Printed in the United States of America

ISBN 0-940847-07-8

Library of Congress Catalog Card: 86-90578

ACKNOWLEDGEMENTS

I wish to thank the experts and leaders in the fields of Natural Family Planning and Reproductive Physiology who have so kindly read over portions of this manuscript: Dr. Edward Keefe, Rev. Paul Marx, O.S.B., Rita Henry-Breault, Gilles Breault, Dr. Claude Lanctot, Mrs. Emmi Vollman, Dr. Robert Jackson, Suzannah Cooper, Mrs. Rose Fuller, and Dr. Joel Hargrove. They generously gave of their time and expertise, and for this I am most grateful.

I also want to thank all of the women and couples I have counseled over the years. They were my teachers, and gave me information I could obtain nowhere else.

This work has benefitted tremendously from the careful and literate influence of my editor, my mother, Marjorie Shore. Thank you, Mom, it wouldn't be the same without your help.

Finally, I want to sincerely thank Jeanne Kahan for her beautiful and sensitive illustrations. Her drawings combine medical accuracy with a feminine beauty and gentleness that reflect her own nature.

Figure 1. Rudolf F. Vollman, M.D.

This book is lovingly
DEDICATED
to
RUDOLF F. VOLLMAN, M.D.
1912-1985
and his devoted wife
Emmi Vollman
in deepest appreciation
for
their work and inspiration

CONTENTS

ILLUSTRATIONS

PREFACE

I have approached this work with love and excitement. It is now over a decade since the publication of my first book on this subject.[1]

In the late 1960s and early 70s many of my generation (the post-war baby boom) were having second thoughts about some of the technical advances in birth control along with their concerns about the environment, nuclear war, chemicals in the food supply, and so on. There arose a spontaneous desire for more intimate bodily self-awareness and a natural, safe and self-directed method of birth control.

Long before the emergence of this "au naturel" subculture of the baby boom generation that I was addressing in my first book, the main group espousing a natural, non-chemical, non-invasive form of family planning was the Catholic Church. For theological reasons, Catholic physicians and lay people developed methods they later came to call "Natural Family Planning". The only other people interested in physical signs of fertility were medical doctors dealing with the problem of infertility. They too developed a science of fertility detection based on basal temperature and cyclical changes in the cervical mucus.

When I wrote my first book on natural birth control, all of my information was derived from the latter group. I am sorry to admit that I knew nothing of the Catholic research and involvement with basal temperature, etc. I had the mistaken but widespread impression that the Catholic Church only sanctioned "rhythm". I had been personally involved in an infertility workup of many years duration, and had been taught to take my temperature and watch for "Spinnbarkeit" mucus discharge, as the doctors called it. I thought I was very clever to turn this information around for purposes of birth control. To document natural signs of fertility, I researched medical journals on the life span of sperm and egg and the correlation of the Spinnbarkeit mucus with fertility. I utilized the World Health Organization report *Biology of Fertility Control by Periodic Abstinence*[2] for a definition of "high" temperatures.

After publication of my book, I learned that the Catholic Church had a highly scientific, well developed body of information on this method; that the Rhythm Method was old news and out of favor; that they had combination methods similar to mine, mucus alone methods, and even self examination of the cervix. Fortunately, I had arrived at the same conclusions and virtually the same rules from my infertility research and WHO sources. We were, after all, dealing with the same physiology. I want to acknowledge here the tremendous pioneering work of the Catholic Church in documenting the natural signs of fertility. It was their studies that formed the basis for the WHO report on periodic abstinence.

This book is a non-sectarian presentation of the principles of non-invasive, healthful and natural birth control. I hope it will be useful to all reading it, whatever their background. Whether you are following your conscience or pursuing a more natural lifestyle in our highly technical society, this book is for you with love.

Margaret Nofziger
Nashville, Tennessee, 1988

CHAPTER 1

INTRODUCTION TO NATURAL BIRTH CONTROL

Choosing and planning the size of one's family is a major consideration in the lives of most people. Few couples are willing or able to raise an unlimited number of children. The birth of each child has tremendous impact on the family. Ideally it is an event which is carefully and consciously planned.

In our modern technological society, most women of childbearing age have used, or known about, artificial and hormonal means of family planning. Some segments of our diverse population follow personal moral values in choosing the means to limit the size of their families. Others are repelled by the "high tech" aspects of modern life and seek a natural, safe, holistic approach.

Who is interested in natural birth control? People from many cultural backgrounds and with varying motivations:

- The health conscious who do not want to interfere chemically, mechanically, or through synthetic hormones with their bodily processes
- Individuals observing religious or ethical commitments
- Anti-technologists seeking peaceful co-existence with nature
- Feminists retaining complete control over their bodies
- Consumer advocates demanding a say in all aspects of their health care

Natural birth control is best practiced by committed, monogamous, stable couples. Permanent couples can best learn and apply the physical and mental subtleties that make this method work.

The basis of natural birth control is the physiological fact that conception can only take place for about four to six days of a woman's menstrual cycle. The parameters of those fertile days are determined by the functional lifespan of sperm (3 - 5 days of fertility before ovulation) and the ovum (1 day of fertility after ovulation). At this stage of our knowledge we cannot presume to know the day of ovulation, but must, instead, look for the beginning and end of the fertile phase of the cycle which will be 7 to 12 days. There are physical signs throughout a woman's menstrual cycle that can reveal the approach of the fertile period and its passing:

1. The basal (waking) temperature is low before and higher after ovulation.
2. A clear, profuse, slippery mucus discharge is present at the vagina before, and at the time of, ovulation.
3. The cervix of the uterus goes through distinct changes as the cycle progresses from infertile to fertile to infertile again.
4. The length of each cycle can help predict the time of ovulation. The timespan between ovulation and the following menstrual period is relatively stable at about two weeks. This consistency provides the basis for an "Early Days" formula based on past cycle length to help determine the days of infertility before ovulation.
5. There are also secondary signs of fertility including intermenstrual (midcycle) pain, breast tenderness, and changes in mood and libido.

This book will elaborate on these natural signs of fertility, outline rules for birth control based on these signs, and explain the physiology behind them. Statistics on artificial and natural birth control are provided for comparison and a general idea of the effectiveness that can be expected. I have included some historical background on natural family planning for perspective. This book is intended for use by diverse groups interested in a natural approach, whatever their background or motivation. It can provide an added source of information when used within the context of formal classes, or it can be the basis for personal study.

It is wise to observe and record as many of the different signs of fertility as possible. The periodic *changes* in body temperature, cervical mucus, cervix and number of days between menstrual periods should all correlate for maximum accuracy in estimating the fertile and infertile phases of the menstrual cycle.

Some natural family planning organizations teach and encourage the use of progressive changes in cervical mucus as a reliable method and believe that other observations may detract and confuse. I disagree. In my experience, the mucus symptom alone does not provide effectiveness ratings comparable to the combination of methods. (Please refer to Chapter 11 – Studies and Statistics). While this select method may have its place in underdeveloped countries, I cannot recommend this approach if other signs can be noted.

Natural birth control may not appeal to everyone since it entails detailed record keeping and periodic abstinence during fertile periods. However, to those who seek it out, it can be a rewarding adventure, a means of deeper commitment and communication, and a path to feminine self-esteem through self knowledge.

4

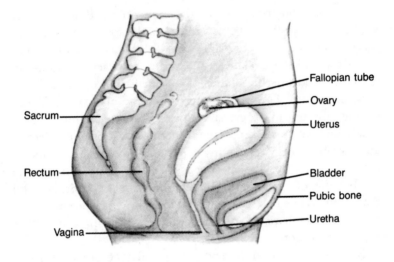

Fallopian tube
Ovary
Uterus
Sacrum
Bladder
Pubic bone
Rectum
Uretha
Vagina

Figure 2.   Side view of female pelvis

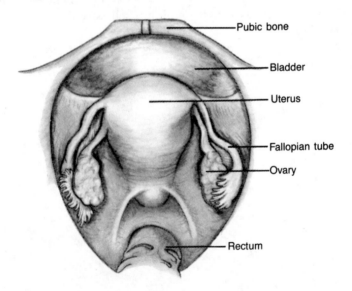

Pubic bone
Bladder
Uterus
Fallopian tube
Ovary
Rectum

Figure 3. Top view of female pelvis.

CHAPTER 2

PHYSIOLOGY OF REPRODUCTION

In practicing this method of birth control which is derived from women's natural signs of fertility, it is immensely helpful to have a good understanding of female physiology that creates the signs that we observe. I could put the simple rules of natural birth control in a tidy little brochure and save you a lot of study, but understanding *why* is important for correct application of the rules, and empowers you as a woman. The workings of your reproductive system are intricate, but do not have to be a mystery.

A woman's reproductive system is much more complex than a man's, as it progressively changes on a cyclic basis. A woman moves in and out of a state of fertility with a regular rhythm. It is this periodic fertility and infertility in a woman's menstrual cycle that forms the basis for natural birth control.

In this chapter you will learn about basic physiology of the female reproductive organs; the interplay of female hormones with their effect on body temperature and the cervix of the uterus; and relevant characteristics of sperm and egg.

FEMALE REPRODUCTIVE ORGANS

The female reproductive system consists of the uterus (womb), a pear-shaped organ; the cervix, which is at the lower, smaller end of the uterus; the vagina, a pleated tunnel leading from the cervix of the uterus to the outside of the body at the vulva (external genitalia); and the two ovaries and fallopian tubes. The mucus lining of the uterus, called the endometrium, the breasts, the fallopian tubes and the cervix react to hormones from the ovaries, and the activity of the ovaries is stimulated by hormones from the pituitary gland located at the base of the brain. During a phase of the menstrual cycle the endometrium of the uterus becomes thick and spongy. Breasts become heavy and tender. Fertility signs abound. The cervix rises and falls in the pelvis, producing a differing quality and quantity of mucus, becoming more and less receptive to sperm. The fallopian tubes move the egg toward the uterus with motion of their cilia and peristaltic action of the muscular layer of the tube. Muscular activity of the tube is influenced by hormones and is highest at the time of ovulation when the flower-like fimbriated end of the fallopian tube nearest the active ovary actually reaches around the ovary and catches the egg like a catcher's mitt! (See Figure 5). The female reproductive organs go through their phases of fertility and infertility based on signals from endocrine hormones produced in the ovary and pituitary gland.

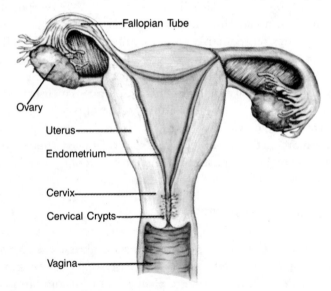

Figure 4.   Female reproductive organs.

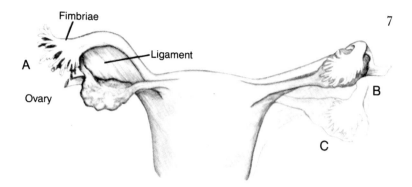

Figure 5. Movements of the tube and ovary. (A) Tube extended; no movement, (B) Contraction begins; tube curves around ovary. (C) Strong contraction of ligaments; ovary rotates, fimbriae cover ovary.

REPRODUCTIVE ENDOCRINE HORMONES

There is feedback of information and instruction among the reproductive glands of the endocrine system. First, due to low estrogen levels in the bloodstream at the time of the period, the hypothalamus (part of the brain, not an endocrine gland), which is situated right next to the pituitary gland, sends GnRH (Gonadotropin Releasing Hormone) to the anterior (front) pituitary gland. This hormone causes the anterior pituitary gland to secrete FSH – Follicle Stimulating Hormone. As the name implies, the hormone FSH stimulates the follicles, egg sacs within the ovaries, to ripen. Six to sixteen follicles start to develop[1] and they, in turn, produce estrogen, an ovarian hormone. Soon, one follicle, called the Graafian follicle, dominates and the others recede. Rising blood levels of estrogen cause the cervix to produce fertile cervical mucus. Estrogen also causes the endometrial lining of the uterus to increase. This is called the "proliferative stage" of the cycle. This enhanced endometrium will nourish an embryo in the event of conception. Around two weeks before the period, very high levels of estrogen circulating in the bloodstream provide feedback to the pituitary to send a surge of LH (Leutinizing Hormone),[2] also produced by the anterior pituitary gland. High estrogen levels then signal the pituitary to stop sending FSH[3] which

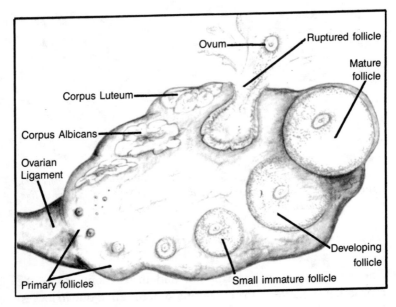

Ovum

Ruptured follicle

Mature follicle

Corpus Luteum

Corpus Albicans

Ovarian Ligament

Developing follicle

Primary follicles

Small immature follicle

Figure 6.   Life cycle of the Graffian follicle.

has reached its peak at this time.[4] The rise in LH causes ovulation to occur within 12 to 24 hours of the LH peak.[5,6] The day of the LH surge is the most fertile day of the cycle.[7]

After the egg is released from the ovary, the small crater from whence it came becomes a temporary endocrine gland called the *corpus luteum* (yellow body). Right after ovulation, the corpus luteum occupies ⅓ to ½ of the ovary.[8] This temporary gland secretes a hormone called progesterone. Progesterone inhibits the

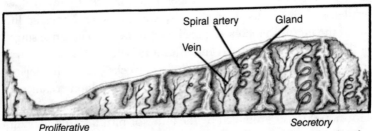

Spiral artery   Gland

Vein

Proliferative

Secretory

Figure 7.   Progressive changes of the endometrium during the menstrual cycle.

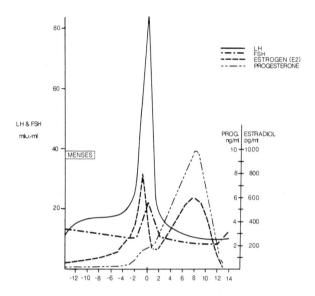

Figure 8. Plasma levels of FSH, LH, Estrogen (E₂) and Progesterone during the human menstrual cycle. Redrawn from Speroff L, Vande Wiele RL. Regulation of the human menstrual cycle. Am J Obstet Gynecol 109:234,1971. With permission.

action of estrogen on the endometrium.[1] At this point, the *proliferative* phase is over and the *secretory* (luteal) phase begins. The follicle is no longer producing estrogen, but the corpus luteum produces a small amount of estrogen along with the progesterone. Progesterone and estrogen cause a rapid buildup of the endometrium in preparation for nourishment and housing of a potential embryo. Progesterone also causes production of a dense, obstructive cervical mucus and a rise in basal (at rest) body temperature. This rise in temperature occurs about two days after the LH surge.[4]

The corpus luteum has a productive life span of only about two weeks. Progesterone decreases LH production by negative feedback and the corpus luteum shrivels up and becomes a scar on the ovary. This scar is called the corpus albicans (white body). At this point, estrogen and progesterone levels fall off and no longer maintain the thick, rich lining of the uterus, which is then sloughed off in menstruation, and the whole process begins again.

That wasn't so bad, was it?

EGG AND SPERM

At birth, baby girls already possess in their tiny ovaries all of the primary oocytes (immature eggs) they will ever have – 300,000 to 500,000 in number! Only about 500 of these will mature into eggs. The egg can barely be seen with the naked eye. It is the size of the head of a small pin, and about 2000 times the size of a sperm which can only be seen under a microscope. Sperm are produced in the testes of the male after puberty. FSH from the pituitary causes spermatogenesis (sperm production).[1] Forty to sixty million reach maturity each day and they are produced continually throughout adult life.

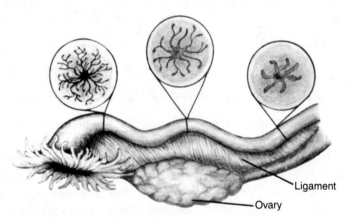

Figure 9.   Cross sections of fallopian tube.

Approximately 200 to 500 million sperm are deposited near the cervix during intercourse.[9] But relatively few ever get to the inner third of the fallopian tube, the site of fertilization. Most are lost to the acid environment of the vagina, or go up the other fallopian tube, or get lost in the uterus. For each sperm in the fallopian tube, there are about 500 in the uterus, 200,000 in the cervical mucus and 10 million in the ejaculate.[10] Many of the sperm are stored in the mucus within crypts in the cervix for gradual release. Those that bypass storage in the crypts and swim straight for the fallopian tube arrive in about five minutes from the moment they are deposited in the vagina.[10]

Sperm have a protein dissolving enzyme in their miniscule "heads" called proteinase, which is necessary to break through a protein barrier on the egg. Interestingly, cervical mucus from the female has a "proteinase inhibitor" which is at its lowest concentration at ovulation when the mucus is displaying several other "sperm-friendly" characteristics.

It is generally accepted that the egg lives only 12 to 24 hours at the most. Although some researchers postulate a five-day sperm survival,[3,11] most biologists working in the field of human reproduction believe that fertilizing capability usually lasts for only about two days,[12,13] three at the most. Sperm have been found alive in favorable mucus for a number of days after intercourse. However, in mammals, sperm generally maintain motility longer than the ability to fertilize an ovum.[13]

THE CERVIX AND ITS MUCUS

There are about 100 mucus producing pockets, or "crypts" in the canal of the cervix.[14] *Secretory* cells lining the crypts produce 20-60 mg of thick, opaque mucus per day during the nonfertile phases of the cycle but increase production to about 600 mg of clear, slick mucus per day at the fertile time around ovulation.[15,16] The cervix also contains about 5% *ciliated* cells[17] whose cilia wave, thus facilitating the downward movement of the mucus flow toward the vagina.[9,18] The thick, sticky type of mucus appears after ovulation under the influence of progesterone, and when estrogen is in short supply. It reappears after the period until rising estrogen levels change it to the more fertile type. This opaque, tacky mucus forms a thick barrier of criss-cross "macromolecules" across the mouth of the cervix which makes it next to impossible for sperm to penetrate. It also contains leucocytes which kill sperm and bacteria, is acidic, and low in glucose.

Fertile mucus produced under the influence of estrogen from the ripening follicle is quite different in appearance and consistency.

It is clear, thin and watery. In its ultimate form it can be stretched as a glistening string between thumb and outstretched forefinger. During the most fertile hours or days of the cycle it has the slippery feel and elasticity of raw egg white. Some women never see this stretchy quality, and instead notice only increased wetness. Both the thin watery and "egg white" mucus are signs of enhanced fertility. *Spinnbarkeit* is the name for the elastic property of this

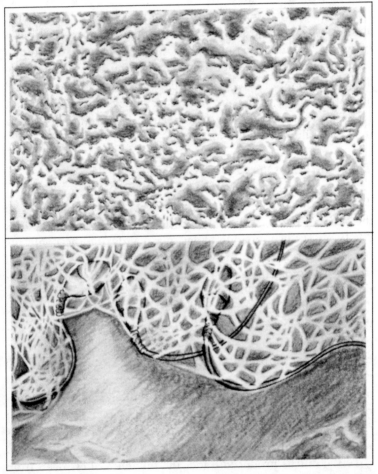

Figure 10. Cervical mucus. (A) dense, impervious cervical mucus; (B) sperm trapped in thick cellular mucus;

fertile gel. It is a German word that physicians and biologists who studied fertility (or infertility) adopted because there was no English equivalent. It means elasticity, the ability to be stretched into fiber-like threads.

Spinnbarkeit, the most fertile sperm-receptive mucus, contains long molecules that lie in rather straight lines oriented in the direction of the cervical canal,[3] all going the same way like combed

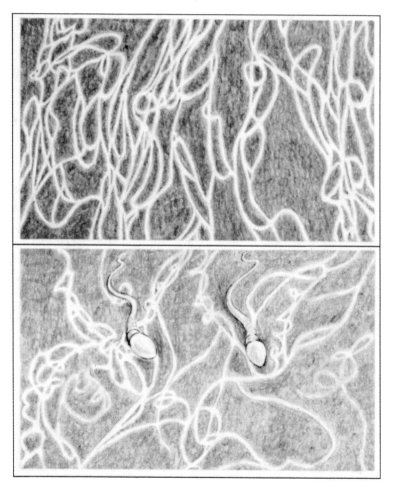

(C) fertile, ovulatory mucus; (D) Sperm moving freely in thin cervical mucus.

hair. There are spaces between these macromolecules which become channels for the sperm to travel in. This type of mucus is friendly and welcoming to sperm. It is alkaline rather than acidic. It guides and nourishes them and orients them upward in their journey to the egg, another miraculous contribution to the continuance of the species. This lubricative fertile mucus, or just the sensation of wetness, is crucial to fertilization. It is imperative to keep sperm far away from it if one is to avoid conception since ovulation occurs very close to the last day of clear, glassy mucus[19] or maximum wetness. If the mucus is stretchy at all, or even just wet and slippery, it is a sign of optimum fertility.

Another property of fertile mucus is crystallization into a fern pattern when dry. Crystallization of mucus is caused by crystals of sodium and potassium forming around organic matter.[18] The ferning pattern can be seen when dried mucus is viewed under a low-power microscope.

The greatest volume of clear fertile mucus occurs simultaneously with the estrogen peak and preceding the rise of LH and ovulation. Maximum ferning and sperm penetration coincide with the LH surge the day after the estrogen peak.[6] The LH peak occurs about 16 hours before ovulation.[5] Mucus can be profuse and liquid for as little as a few hours or as long as six days. Ovulation occurs within hours after the last day of this fertile mucus.[8,20]

The cervix has several ways of helping or hindering sperm migration to the uterus and tubes. It not only produces hostile or friendly mucus, forming a plug at the cervix or clear channels to the egg, but the crypts themselves are important to sperm survival. The vagina is not a friendly place for sperm. It has an acid environment which kills sperm and contains *phagocytes* which are scavenger cells that rapidly remove sperm. If the sperm can get past the entry of the vagina to the cervix (during such times as the mucus is fluid and channeled) they can hide in the cervical crypts and obtain nourishment (energy) to be released in a prolonged, steady supply.[9,21] Sperm do not move from crypt to crypt within the cervix. They are apparently stored in a particular crypt and go from there directly to the uterus. The bulk of sperm deposited in the vagina during the fertile phase move up through the central column of mucus directly to the uterus. Those stored and sustained in the crypts stay there for the first day and then are released up into the uterus the next day.[22] Cervical mucus also filters out dead or defective sperm.[9]

An important function of cervical mucus is as a barrier protecting the uterus from contaminants from the vagina and the outside world during most of the reproductive cycle. The dense mucus present after ovulation also contains leucocytes which destroy bacteria. The cervix and its mucus only allow sperm to enter the uterus at specific short intervals near the time of ovulation in order to allow fertilization and reproduction.

THE MENSTRUAL CYCLE

"A woman does not always menstruate regularly; every so often, the intervals are shorter or longer. After the menarche, as well as in the premenopausal age, there are great irregularities, as there are after childbirth. In addition, such irregularities are produced by diseases, indisposition, malnutrition, and passions."

J.A. Clos, 1858[23]

The menstrual cycle begins with the first day of the menstrual period and ends with the day before the following menstrual period. The first day of the menstrual period is called "day one" of the cycle. This cycle is divided into two segments: the preovulatory (or postmenstrual) phase, and the postovulatory (or premenstrual) phase. The preovulatory phase begins on the first day of menstruation ("day one") and ends at ovulation; the postovulatory phase begins after ovulation and continues through the day before menstruation.

The earlier preovulatory phase can vary in length, while the later postovulatory phase is constant at approximately two weeks. When the cycle is long, it is the preovulatory phase that is long; if short, the preovulatory phase is short.

Figure 11.   Variation in cycle length.

PREOVULATORY	POSTOVULATORY
Long cycle ^	12 to 16 days
Average cycle ^	12 to 16 days
Short cycle ^	11 to 15 days
^ = ovulation	

Variation in cycle length is caused by a delay in FSH secretion to reach a high enough concentration to stimulate the development of the follicles[24] or by an insufficient LH surge. Late ovulation will cause a late menstrual period. Late ovulation is frequently caused by illness, physical or emotional stress, and travel. Stress affects the cycle via the hypothalamus which directs emotions, sleep, body temperature, etc. The cycle can also be disrupted by dieting or constant strenuous exercise, such as distance running, which lowers body fat. Changes in fat to lean ratio interfere with hormone production.

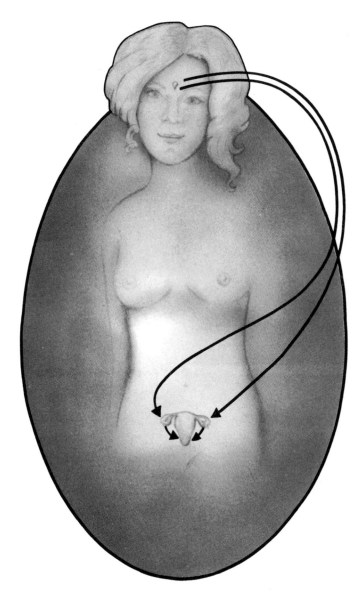

Figure 12. Hormones control the menstrual cycle.

CHAPTER 3

NATURAL SIGNS OF FERTILITY

Principles of natural birth control have been formulated from the physiological processes of the female menstrual cycle about which you have just read.

Endocrine hormones of the female reproductive system establish and maintain the menstrual cycle. They also provide exterior signs and symptoms that we can observe and record. Clues can be assembled and rules applied to ascertain boundaries of the natural fertile phase of the cycle. These rules and formulas will not pinpoint the moment or even the day of ovulation, but rather define the beginning and end of the period of abstinence required to avoid pregnancy.

A record of the waking (basal) temperature forms the basis of this natural method of birth control. A menstrual calendar adds perspective. There are other signs which are to be noted on the temperature chart. When all available natural signs are recorded, they provide an accurate representation of the inner workings of an individual female reproductive cycle.

HISTORICAL RHYTHM - A SOLID FOUNDATION

Rhythm deserves a special place in the discussion of natural birth control. It was the earliest scientific approach to periodic abstinence as a birth control alternative, and the first method of conception regulation accepted by the Catholic Church. Rhythm is still widely practiced in Japan and other countries with good results.

Rhythm is no longer recommended as a freestanding, self-contained method of birth control, but is useful as a tool to educate and familiarize yourself with *your own personal pattern of fertility.* Rhythm is to be studied, but not relied upon, except in conjunction with other signs of fertility.

Rhythm is based on calculations using the length of past cycles. These calculations depend on four assumptions:

1. Ovulation occurs 12-16 days before menstruation.
2. The ovum (egg) lives for 12-24 hours.
3. Sperm are able to fertilize the egg for up to three days.
4. The length of a woman's menstrual cycle is fairly stable.

The first three assumptions have scientific merit and should serve the method well. The fourth, however, is not true of all women and for that reason is probably the cause of unreliability of this method when used alone. Women with irregular cycle length probably contributed most of the unplanned pregnancies resulting from use of the Rhythm Method.

Since menstruation is known to take place approximately two weeks (12 to 16 days) after ovulation, the possible dates of ovulation can be calculated for past cycles, and estimated dates of ovulation set for future cycles. To estimate the parameters of future ovulations, you must keep track of the date of the first day of your menstrual period for at least six, and preferably twelve, months. Next, determine the length of each cycle by counting days from the first day of the period through the *day before* the next period. Note the length of the longest and the shortest cycles in your menstrual history.

After determining the longest and shortest cycles on record, subtract 18 from the shortest cycle to predict the earliest ovulation. Then subtract 11 from the longest cycle to predict the latest ovulation.[1] The resulting two figures give you the span of time within upcoming cycles that you are likely to be fertile. For example:

Shortest cycle in 12 months was 27 days
Longest cycle in 12 months was 30 days
27 − 18 = 9 and 30 − 11 = 19

Days 9 through 19 are potentially fertile, accounting for your history of early and late ovulations. Intercourse must be avoided for this eleven day period to avoid pregnancy.

The early estimated infertile days are somewhat unreliable because sperm might retain their fertilizing capability for more than three days in highly favorable cervical mucus and/or ovulation could be earlier than ever before. The late estimated infertile days can be unreliable because, although 24 hours is the outside limit of ovum survival, ovulation is more likely to be late than early since the ovum requires time to mature[2] and stresses slow it down rather than speed it up. A quirk about late ovulation is that if a woman is going to be late ovulating due to stress, for example, she will either be just a few days late or her body may mysteriously choose to be *two weeks* late for ovulation, putting the big event right around the time of expected menstruation. To further confuse matters, late ovulation may be accompanied by a drop of blood or pink discharge caused by high estrogen concentrations. This can be mistaken for the beginning of menstruation, thus mimicking a "safe" time and encouraging intercourse. That scenario precedes the lament: "I got pregnant the day before my period." Because of late ovulation, her period was due in another two weeks. This pitfall, however, exists only for the woman choosing rhythm alone.

When an "Early Days" rhythm formula is used to establish preovulatory infertile days and basal temperature is added to establish postovulatory infertile days, reliability improves dramatically. By these means the more commonly occurring late ovulation will become evident by a delay in temperature elevation.

In terms of entire populations of couples who use no other method of contraception, the Rhythm Method has its place and can account for a substantial decrease in birth rates. But for the individual woman in most modern societies, its only place is as an "Early Days" adjunct to other natural signs of fertility which are more reliable for determining fertility in the current cycle.

THE BIPHASIC TEMPERATURE CURVE

The cyclic rise and fall of a woman's waking (basal) temperature provides the most reliable objective sign of *natural periodic infertility.* The waking temperature starts out low during the estrogen dominated early phase of the cycle and rises under the influence of progesterone after ovulation has taken place. Because the rise in the waking temperature demonstrates the presence of critical blood levels of progesterone, it can provide assurance that ovulation has indeed passed and the 12-24 hour lifespan of the ovum has run its course. Once ovulation has taken place, it will not happen again during that cycle, and the remainder of the cycle is definitely infertile.

Each morning the waking temperature is noted and a dot is placed on the temperature chart under the appropriate date across from the correct temperature reading. The dots are connected and, in an ovulatory cycle, a "biphasic curve" becomes apparent.

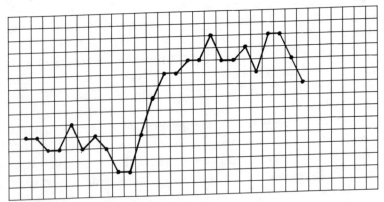

Figure 13. The biphasic temperature curve.
This curve has two distinct phases: a low one and a high one. The temperature will remain high during the second phase and will not usually fall until a day or so before the next menstruation. Ovulation occurs within a range of four days before to two days after the temperature rise.

This objective, reliable sign of the *definitely* infertile phase of a cycle is central to the practice of natural birth control.

INTERPRETING THE MUCUS SIGN

The mucus sign is an excellent outward sign of rising levels of estrogen secreted from the ripening follicle(s). As described in Chapter 2, there are two types of cervical mucus produced by the secretory cells of the cervix: the clear, slippery fertility-enhancing, sperm-friendly mucus; and the dense, obstructive, sperm-blocking mucus. The former is produced under the influence of estrogen; the latter appears after ovulation under the influence of progesterone, and sometimes early in the cycle, right after the menstrual period.

In cycles of average or longer-than-average length, the first few days after the menstrual period may provide a dry sensation at the vagina with no discharge or feeling of wetness. These days are considered "dry" days and have a low probability of conception. However, they cannot be considered positively infertile like the days after the temperature rise. All days in the preovulatory (postmenstrual) phase of the cycle are possibly fertile with the possible exception of the first few days of the menstrual period. If you have short cycles, there may be no early "dry" days. The days toward the end of, and after, the menstrual period should be considered fertile no matter what the state of the mucus for women with short cycles.

Mucus reflecting enhanced fertility is abundant, flowing, transparent, and slippery, often with a stretchy quality called Spinnbarkeit (it is capitalized because it is a German noun). This slick glassy mucus resembles raw egg white in consistency and appearance. It usually builds up in quantity over a few days, starting with a wet sensation and building to a noticeable discharge from the vagina. You may not have enough to gather on your finger and stretch a shimmering thread between your thumb and forefinger; however, if you notice a *lubricative, slippery sensation* at the vulva, note Spinnbarkeit on your temperature chart. The last day of this egg-white mucus correlates closely with the LH surge and ovulation.[3]

After ovulation, fertile type mucus disappears leaving thick, pasty mucus or no mucus at all. This disappearance of fertile mucus will coincide with the temperature shift to the infertile phase.

The dense opaque mucus, which often appears early in the preovulatory phase of the cycle, is sometimes referred to as "infertile mucus." There is really no such thing as infertile mucus in the preovulatory phase of the cycle. This white or yellow tacky mucus is not conducive to sperm. However, it often precedes clear, wet mucus by only a day or two, and that's too close for comfort considering that sperm remain capable of fertilization for three to five days. In the preovulatory (postmenstrual) phase, any form of mucus discharge is to be considered potentially fertile.

It is a helpful habit to check your mucus when you use the bathroom. Some teachers of natural family planning suggest the use of toilet paper to collect the mucus, but some toilet papers can irritate the sensitive tissues in some women when wiping between the labia several times a day rather than just blotting the area after urinating. In this instance, I suggest you gather mucus at the opening of the vagina with a clean finger.

For some women, the mucus sign may only appear for two to three days[4] and will not provide adequate warning of impending ovulation to allow for the lifespan of sperm. In one recent study,[5] 8 of 29 cycles showed only a two day mucus symptom before ovulation (LH surge).

Some natural family planning groups stress the mucus sign as a sole indicator of fertility, establishing the end of the fertile phase as well as the beginning. The main disadvantage to rejecting the temperature sign is the problem of "double peak." The term "peak" refers to the last day of Spinnbarkeit or wet mucus. Ovulation can be delayed, even once the process has begun, by physical, mental or emotional stress. The follicle temporarily stops developing after it has already begun secreting estrogen, which has caused the appearance of fertile mucus. When estrogen suddenly drops off, fertile mucus disappears, mimicking the abrupt cessation of mucus that occurs after ovulation. Intercourse may occur followed by resumption of the ovulatory process, a second batch of mucus, and finally ovulation in the presence of fresh sperm. This "double peak" is not a problem if temperatures are available to confirm the presence of progesterone, which is a more reliable sign of true ovulation.

In observing the mucus sign alone, the Billings Ovulation Method[6] of natural family planning recommends abstinence during the menstrual period and from the first sign of mucus at the vulva through the fourth day after "peak" (the last day of Spinnbarkeit mucus). During the early dry days, intercourse is permitted only on alternate nights to avoid obscuring the mucus sign with seminal fluid. If you wish to rely primarily on the mucus sign, with the other signs as backup, I recommend that you seek personal counseling or a class in this method.

The Billings Ovulation Method has definite advantages for teaching illiterate couples in the developing world and has proven effective in conjunction with *biological breastfeeding* (see Chapter 7) in regulating the frequency of births.

SIGNS OF THE CERVIX

The cervix of the uterus goes through cyclic changes each month in position and consistency under hormonal influence. Dr. Edward Keefe, a New York gynecologist, was the first to document these changes in the cervix during the different phases of the menstrual cycle. In 1962 he requested that some of his patients check their mucus directly from the cervix rather than at the vulva. They thus discovered, and reported to him, that the cervix softened and the os opened to admit the tip of a finger as the cervical mucus became more glassy and abundant.[7] In 1964, Dr. Keefe asked his patients to also note the elevation of their cervix as low, high, or very high when they checked for opening, softening and an increase in Spinnbarkeit. They noted that the cervix was low in the vaginal canal during the infertile phases of the cycle and highest at the fertile time as indicated by the mucus and temperatures.[8] In 1978, the Serena organization of Canada began teaching that the uterine cervix often has a tilt toward the posterior wall of the vagina during the infertile phase and is straighter in the vaginal canal during the days surrounding ovulation.[9]

The cervix is the source of fertile mucus. At the same time that one observes an increase or decrease in cervical mucus, the cervical os (opening) opens and closes. As it dilates under the influence of estrogen, it also becomes soft, in contrast to its otherwise firm condition (soft like lips, firm like nose). The uterus, and therefore the cervix of the uterus, changes position in the pelvis because of the action of estrogen on the uterine ligaments. High levels of estrogen make these supporting ligaments taut, drawing the uterus higher and straighter in the body. Dr. Keefe calls this change in position of the cervix the "cephalad shift."[8]

After menstruation and after ovulation, the cervix will be found low in the vaginal canal, relatively easy to reach for inspection with the first two fingers of one hand. It will feel firm and rather dry, with the os closed. The os will contain a plug of thick mucus which is not easily felt. The closed os feels like a dimple and the examining finger cannot enter.

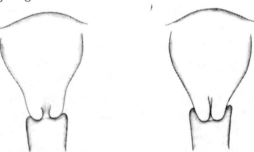

Figure 14. Changes of the cervix. (A) Fertile cervix: high, open. (B) Infertile cervix: low, closed

As ovulation approaches, the cervix begins to soften and the os gradually opens over the course of about five days. This coincides with the beginning of the mucus discharge and is also caused by rising levels of estrogen. Just prior to ovulation the os will expand so that your finger tip can slide into it about ¼ to ½ inch if you have had children. The cervix will feel soft and wet with fertile mucus. The cephalad shift will place the cervix high in the body, making it more inaccessible than before, and rather difficult to reach.

When checking the cervix, you can squat, sit on the toilet, or stand with back curled forward and one foot on a stool or chair. The uterus is folded forward with the cervix pushed against the back wall of the vaginal canal. You will reach toward your backbone to find it. If you cannot immediately reach the cervix, try pressure from above with the other hand. It is there, keep trying.

A good time to check the cervix is in the morning, perhaps at the first visit to the bathroom. Be sure your fingernails and hands are washed. To examine the cervix, insert the first two fingers of one hand into the vagina. When you find the cervix, feel for firmness or softness, the size of the os, and highness or lowness.

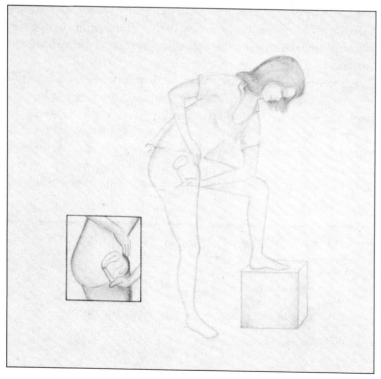

Figure 15. Woman inspecting her cervix. This illustration is redrawn and used with permission of Dr. Edward F. Keefe and Linacre Laboratories, makers of the Ovulindex® thermometer, the only thermometer accurate to 0.1°F at 98°F.

Before withdrawing the fingers, gently grasp the cervix between them and slide the fingers down and over the tip of the cervix with a slight pressure to squeeze any mucus out of the cervical os and onto your fingers for inspection of the cervical mucus gathered at its source. This internal collection of mucus is important to evaluate the *current* mucus sample.

There are no absolute rules available for abstinence with the cervix as the major indicator of fertility. At present, the cervix sign is not used alone. It is valuable to compare the state of the cervix with other major signs so that it may confirm and augment them. Early in the cycle, you can assume that *any change* toward opening, softening, or secretion of mucus indicates potential fertility even if there is dryness at the vulva and/or the "Early Days" rule indicates infertility. The closing and lowering of the cervix confirms, but does not supersede, a sustained rise in temperature as the indicator of infertility.

Some women may have a cultural or personal aversion to this intimate examination. While it is not mandatory, it can be very helpful, especially during lactation or premenopause, when the cervix is a more reliable indicator of approaching ovulation than vulval mucus alone.[10] Also, women with long preovulatory phases can find this approach helpful. For women to whom it is acceptable, the cervix exam can provide a wealth of information.

SUMMARY OF CERVIX SIGNS:

FERTILE	INFERTILE
rising in the pelvis	lowering in the pelvis
open	closed
soft	firm
wet	dry

OTHER SIGNS OF FERTILITY

There are several lesser signs of fertility that deserve mention and, when added to the temperature chart, confirm and enhance the major signs that form the basis of natural birth control. These signs are: (1) intermenstrual pain, (2) postovulatory breast tenderness, (3) fluid retention and weight gain, (4) changes in libido, (5) vulvar swelling, and (6) acne flareups.

INTERMENSTRUAL PAIN, also known as Mittelschmerz, or midcycle pain, is a sharp pain in the lower abdomen near the time of ovulation. The pain can be subtle and fleeting, or so severe that it causes one to double over. This pain was thought to be associated with rupture of the follicle and resulting fluid in the peritoneal cavity, which can cause pain. Dr. Vollman thought that this pain was from smooth muscle contractions in the tubes, uterus and uterine ligaments caused by high levels of estrogen.[11] An ultrasound study[12] found Mittelschmerz to occur right before ovulation and confirmed Dr. Vollman's opinion that it was smooth muscle contraction. However, this study attributed it to the LH surge which, they said, increases contractability of smooth muscle fibers within the ovary itself. Not all women have this reaction to the hormones, but if you do, note it on your chart. If you have never noticed it before, try to pay special attention to sensations in the lower abdomen at the time you expect ovulation and note all such symptoms on your chart. Listen to your body carefully, and you will probably be able to incorporate this important sign into your personal study.

BREAST DISCOMFORT or heaviness is a very reliable sign that ovulation has passed and you are in the progesterone dominated phase of the cycle. After ovulation, and often increasing until the following menstrual period, the breasts can feel sore, swollen and heavy. Hartman[13] attributed this condition to the presence of progesterone from the corpus luteum. This sign will be confirmed by the rise in temperature. Often the breasts will become quite lumpy and tender in the premenstrual phase. This is especially true of women who suffer from fibrocystic disease, a benign condition of the breasts. Fibrocystic disease often responds favorably to the elimination of caffeine and chocolate from the diet. This will usually offer substantial relief and make it a milder symptom.

FLUID RETENTION AND WEIGHT GAIN occur frequently in the postovulatory phase of the cycle, especially noticeable in the days preceding and first day or two of the menstrual period.[14] Often there is a slight increase in weight and a bloated feeling around ovulation. Premenstrual fluid retention can cause a weight gain of 2-10 pounds. If weight gain and discomfort are severe, try to avoid salty foods in this phase of the cycle. Do not take diuretics. Note this weight gain and bloated feeling on your chart for confirmation of ovulation and early warning on the next menstrual period.

CHANGE IN LIBIDO is a useful sign for many women, and a warning to be careful and listen to your brain, not your body, if you want to avoid pregnancy. The rise and fall of hormones often create an increased interest in sex at the time of ovulation and a decreased interest during the postovulatory phase, with renewed interest right before the menstrual period. This very subjective sign has been confirmed by several studies.[15,16] There are hormonal reasons for this pattern of sexual receptiveness and interest. The presence of estrogen increases libido,[17,18] while high levels of progesterone decrease or suppress sexual arousal.[15] Estrogen also increases the small amounts of androgens (male hormones) produced in women by the adrenal glands, and increased androgen enhances the sex drive.[19,20,21,22] Many lower animals have an *estrus cycle* and go into "heat" at their fertile time. A little bleeding accompanies "heat" and the female only permits mating at that time. The cervical mucus flow may be the human equivalent of the "heat" of the *estrus cycle* of animals. Increased libido at ovulation is an interesting natural instinct. Note any changes in sexual desire on your chart. You may well see a pattern. If you find yourself trying to rationalize sex at a fertile time, watch out. It may be the work of this special sign of fertility.

VULVAR SWELLING and aching is a symptom that many women notice around ovulation as well as before and during the menstrual period. Pay close attention at the height of the mucus symptom and see if you notice a heavy, swollen feeling in the inner lips of the vagina (labia minora), sometimes the entire vulva. This symptom will pass after ovulation, and may again be noticeable at the time of the menstrual period. Sometimes aching accompanies the swelling and may require aspirin or another anti-inflammatory agent for relief.

CHAPTER 4

RULES FOR DETERMINING THE FERTILE PERIOD

ESTABLISHING INFERTILITY DURING THE PREMENSTRUAL (POSTOVULATORY) PHASE OF THE CYCLE

Infertile days available for intercourse in the premenstrual (postovulatory) phase of the cycle are quite reliable and relatively easy to determine.

The waking (basal) temperature is the sign employed to establish this infertile segment of the cycle. The temperature is taken every morning upon awakening. Under the influence of estrogen, temperatures will be relatively low. With secretion of progesterone after ovulation, temperatures will rise .4 to .8 (four to eight tenths) of a degree Fahrenheit. Once the temperature maintains this higher plateau for three days, infertility is certain.

The "Strict Temperature Method" allows intercourse only during this premenstrual (postovulatory) part of the cycle. The "Strict" method is the most effective of the natural methods. It does not allow intercourse during the early phase of the cycle after the menstrual period, before ovulation, when there is always some degree of risk. The "Strict Temperature Method" should be used when there are compelling reasons for avoiding pregnancy.

For a rise in waking temperature to be significant, it must climb .4°F (four tenths of a degree) above the preceding six low temperatures within 48 hours. This criteria was established by the World Health Organization Task Force on Methods for Determination of the Fertile Period[1] in 1966. (Some groups such as Serena in Canada set the higher level at .1°F over a coverline placed .1°F above the highest of the low temperatures.[2]) When the temperature has remained .4°F higher than preovulatory lows for three days, intercourse is permitted on that third evening. The third morning of high temperatures should theoretically be infertile, and Serena Canada has fine statistics allowing use of the third morning. However, on the outside chance of a second ovulation within 12 hours due to fraternal twins, this book recommends waiting until the third evening.

According to the WHO Task Force, about 80% of all women will experience an abrupt rise in temperature.[1] Others will record a slow rise over several days, stairstepping or zigzagging up gradually. In this circumstance, Marshall[3] recommends allowing five days of a rise before intercourse.

IN SUMMARY:

The premenstrual (postovulatory) infertile phase begins on the evening of the third waking temperature that is .4°F higher than the six previous low temperatures. In the event of a slow rise, the fifth evening after the beginning of the rise is infertile.

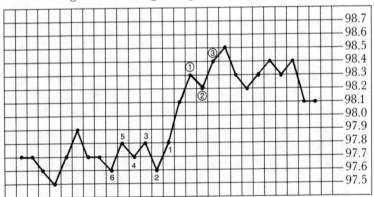

Figure 16. Establishing the high temperature infertile phase

35

Examples:

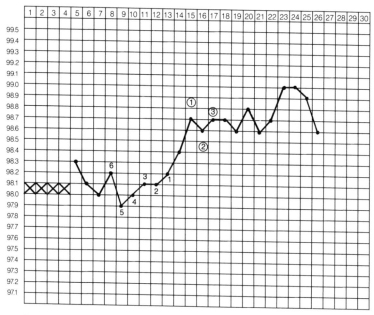

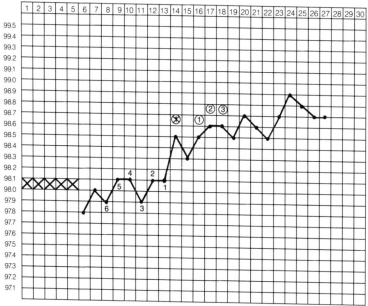

ESTABLISHING INFERTILITY DURING THE POSTMENSTRUAL (PREOVULATORY) PHASE OF THE CYCLE

"EARLY DAYS" FORMULA:

Shortest cycle minus 20 equals first fertile day

This "Early Days" Formula is derived from the original Ogino Rhythm Formula. The enduring principle of the Rhythm System is that ovulation takes place form the 12th to the 16th day *before* the onset of the menstrual period. Because of this consistency we can attempt to predict the time of future ovulation on the basis of a record of previous cycle length. Ogino stated that the first fertile day in the postmenstrual phase could be found by subtracting 18 from the length of the shortest past cycle.[4]

The "Early Days" Formula used in this book adds an extra two days of abstinence to provide for the possibility of a longer sperm life.

If a 27 day cycle was the shortest cycle recorded in 12 months, then Shortest − 27 = 7. Day seven would be the first fertile day, and days 1 - 6 would be available for intercourse. If the shortest recorded cycle was as short as 25 or 26 days in length, only the first four or five days of the cycle, during the menstrual period, would be available for intercourse. If you have short cycles, the early part of the cycle will include very few if any days for sexual contact. This is as it should be because short cycled women are vulnerable to pregnancy due to early ovulation.

Any days deemed infertile by this "Early Days" Formula are subject to confirmation by the absence of the mucus sign and an infertile cervix (see Chapter 3).

It is best to apply this formula with a menstrual history (record of the first day of each period) of 12 months. With cycle dates from 12 previous cycles, the next three cycles have a 90% probability of being within the range of those twelve.[1]

The days of the menstrual period and a few beyond are, for women with long cycles, days of relative infertility and may be used for intercourse. But any sexual contact before a sustained rise in temperature carries some degree of risk. We are still not certain of the length of time that sperm can survive in the favorable environment of the cervical crypts with their sustaining mucus. It is generally accepted that sperm live two to three days, but some biologists believe five days to be the maximum.[5] Also, ovulation usually takes place around the 13th day before the menstrual period, but it can take place as *early* as the 16th day before menstruation. Also, women with long cycles can have an occasional short one with early ovulation. The combination of possible five day sperm viability and early ovulation and/or a long luteal phase of 15 or 16 days makes any apparently infertile day in this phase of the cycle *relatively* infertile. If you have a history of long cycles, you may choose to apply the "Early Days" Formula, mucus observation and cervical signs to establish some days for intercourse during and after the menstrual period. But remember, *if you have a medical or other serious need to avoid pregnancy, if you require effectiveness comparable to oral contraceptives, please use only the "Strict Temperature Method."*

IN SUMMARY:

The preovulatory phase is a very dangerous time in terms of unintended pregnancy. It takes utmost care to *ever* have intercourse during this time when an ovum is ripening. The character of mucus can change quickly from thick and cloudy to wet and clear. The only time to consider intercourse in the preovulatory phase is when:

1. the "Early Days" Formula allows you to do so because of a history of long cycles
2. mucus is absent
3. the cervix displays infertile properties

In the method of natural birth control presented in this book, assured infertility begins on the evening of the 3rd elevated waking temperature. A secondary period of *relative* infertility extends from the first day of the menstrual period through those days designated infertile by the "Early Days" Formula *backed up by observation of cervical mucus* (preferably gathered at the cervix) and by the infertile state of the cervix itself.

NATURAL BIRTH CONTROL AFTER ORAL CONTRACEPTIVES

It can take three to six months for cycles to return to normal after discontinuing birth control pills. The cycles can be longer or shorter than usual, and the length of the luteal phase can be abnormal. Mucus and cervix patterns will probably be disrupted. This is a time for caution. The temperature should be the primary indicator of infertility for three months. Use the "Strict" Temperature Method, and wait for intercourse until the fourth morning of high temperatures.

CHAPTER 5

DOCTOR VOLLMAN'S RULE

Rudolf Vollman was an obstetrician-gynecologist, academic researcher, and statistician who was one of the early scientists to link fertility to basal temperature in the 1930s.

He was born, raised and educated in Germany. He fled Nazi persecution as a young student and resided in Switzerland where he met and married his Swiss wife Emmi and completed his medical studies. In 1952 they went to the United States and in 1958, became American citizens. He was appointed Head of Obstetrics, Perinatal Branch of the National Institute of Health in 1959. In 1972, the Vollmans returned to Switzerland.

Rudolf and Emmi Vollman began their research on the menstrual cycle in the 1930s. Dr. Vollman asked his patients, and Emmi asked her women friends, to keep a menstrual calendar and other notes on their general health. They took their waking temperatures daily. From this evidence he concluded that the Basal Body Temperature (BBT) was an accurate indicator of ovulation. In exploring the early medical literature on the menstrual cycle, he found the papers of T.H. van de Velde and Mary Putnam Jacobi which confirmed his observations. Several scientists were independently coming to the same conclusions in different parts of Europe at the same time. (See Chapter 11, Historical Aspects.)

The Vollmans studied 691 women through 31,645 menstrual cycles over a period of more than 40 years. They knew these women. He counseled many of them in natural family planning based on his own temperature rule. Emmi meticulously graphed and interpreted the data sent each month by these patients. The women would receive a monthly card instructing them on the parameters of their fertility for the coming month. Many of the women kept temperature data for their whole reproductive lives. Some went beyond into the years of menopause. Many taught their daughters to keep these records, often from *before* their first menstrual period. The late Dr. Carl G. Hartman, famous researcher in reproduction said of Rudolf Vollman's voluminous data base: "The world may never again see such willing collaboration between investigator and human subject."[1]

Rudolf Vollman was very active in the natural family planning movement. He helped provide medical and academic credence to this ethics-based system of family planning. He made a major contribution to medical literature about the female reproductive system with his book *The Menstrual Cycle*.[2] Emmi Vollman drew all of the outstanding graphs and figures in this highly technical book.

Rudolf Vollman was a proponent of the Basal Temperature Method of natural family planning. He promoted the "Strict" Temperature Method as being scientifically sound and close to 100% effective. His own temperature rule determined the postovulatory infertile phase by averaging the temperatures from the previous cycle and placing a line on the current chart at that average temperature. After recording four temperatures on or above that average line, the woman could consider herself infertile for the remainder of that cycle.

Concerning early, preovulatory infertile days, Dr. Vollman considered them to be *relatively* infertile at best. He felt that women's cycles were ultimately variable with the constant possibility of a short cycle with accompanying early ovulation. He thought that if one only collected enough cycle data, all possibilities would be fulfilled, all early days would provide some percentage of risk. He had great faith in the objective sign of the Basal Body Temperature in indicating the presence of progesterone in the bloodstream, but he always warned that any day in the preovulatory phase was potentially fertile and the use of those days for intercourse was a calculated risk.

He knew of the mucus symptom of estrogen buildup, but did not think it was exact enough to prevent conception in the preovulatory phase in all cases. He preferred the use of an "Early Days Formula" when women requested some early days for intercourse. He recommended the formula: Shortest Cycle minus 20 for the first fertile day of the cycle. He felt more comfortable with a mathematical, statistical model than with a subjective sign that might not give enough warning for the days of sperm viability.

THE RULE:

> Infertility begins on the fourth morning of a rise
> in temperature on or above the line representing
> the mean temperature of the previous cycle.

To calculate the mean temperature from the previous cycle, add all temperatures from the cycle and divide the total by the number of temperatures. Draw a line on the new chart at that mean (average) temperature and postpone intercourse until the temperatures stay on or above that line for four mornings in a row. The Vollmans found that an individual's mean temperature could remain the same for months or years. This is partly because they dealt with the Centigrade scale which has much larger units of .1° than does the Fahrenheit scale. It took a larger increase in body heat for the temperature to move a full tenth of a degree than it did with the Fahrenheit thermometer. Even with the Fahrenheit thermometer, the average temperature for a whole cycle remains remarkably stable month after month when rounded off to the nearest tenth of a degree. The Vollmans did note, from their extensive data, that the mean temperature gradually falls over the years. As Rudolf Vollman would say with a twinkle in his eye: "When women get older, they get colder." When averaging according to Dr. Vollman's temperature rule, it is acceptable to ignore a temperature that is more than .5° higher or lower than the one before it. He considers it to be an artifact and allows it to be left out of the averaging. If you had 27 temperatures and one spiked up .5° or more from the previous day, figure your average with 26 temperatures.

42

Examples:

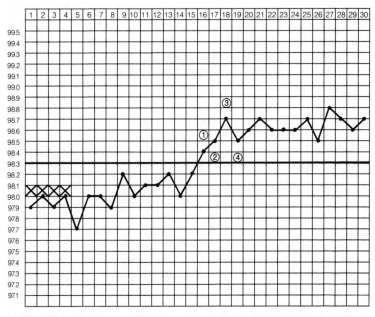

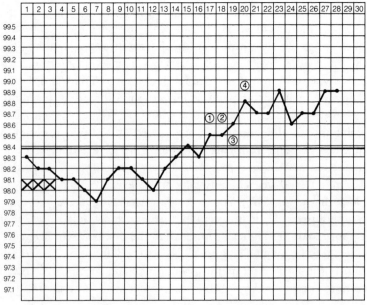

CHAPTER 6

TAKING YOUR TEMPERATURE

THERMOMETERS

Ordinary fever thermometers are not suitable for recording basal (waking) temperatures. A Fahrenheit fever thermometer registers temperatures from 94° to 106°. Each line on the thermometer represents .2° (two tenths of a degree), ie. 98.2°, 98.4°, 98.6°, etc. A special "ovulation" ("basal") thermometer is available which has a range of 96° to 100° with a line for each tenth of a degree. This expanded scale of the relevant temperatures is more accurate and easier to read. When using a mercury thermometer, you will need to shake it down the night before and leave it in place for a full five minutes.

In the last several years, there has emerged on the market an electronic digital thermometer. This thermometer records the temperature digitally in single tenths of a degree and takes only about a minute to register the temperature. An important advantage is that it is not made of glass and does not contain mercury. Inexpensive models are often inaccurate and I have found them to record different temperatures when I repeat the procedure in quick succession. Better brands are more reliable and most sound a little beep when the temperature is measured. It is advisable to take your temperature one minute beyond the beep (or highest reading).

WHEN TO TAKE YOUR TEMPERATURE

You should take your temperature upon awakening each morning before getting out of bed, drinking or smoking. If you are too sleepy to record the reading on the chart, then have a notepad on your night table with dates written in so you can jot it down and record it on your chart later. Do not leave the thermometer to read later as the mercury in an ovulation thermometer could rise due to conditions in the room. An electronic digital thermometer will automatically shut off after a few minutes.

You should take your temperature every day starting with Day 6 of the cycle. If you usually have cycles under 24 days, start taking your temperature on Day 3. If you usually have cycles over 32 days, you can wait until Day 10 to begin taking your temperature. For the first six months take your temperature until the end of the cycle so you will become familiar with the biphasic curve. Later, if you wish, you can stop taking your temperature after five days of elevated readings; seven if it was a gradual climb.

If you use Dr. Vollman's Rule, you should record the entire cycle to calculate the mean (average). Later, after you observe your cycles for four to six months, you can drop four or five days at each end and average the temperatures from the middle weeks of the cycle. However, you must take your temperature for at least 75% of the cycle if you use Dr. Vollman's Rule.

I suggest you take your temperature every morning from the sixth day through the end of the cycle. It is not a lot of trouble and your personal record of temperature and other observations can be very interesting. Patterns emerge. Signs correlate. You can use your chart like a scientific diary. By recording temperature, mucus, mood changes, sex interest, breast symptoms, travel, stress, and other factors from your daily life, you will get to know yourself better. This will, in turn, help you accept your physical and emotional changes through understanding. You will also instill better habits in recording your signs if you do it all through the cycle. It's a small price to pay for a lot of information.

WHERE TO TAKE YOUR TEMPERATURE

Most teachers of natural family planning and physicians treating infertility advise that the temperature be taken rectally for the most reliable readings. Oral temperatures are generally considered to be unreliable because the mouth is subject to fluctuations in temperature from talking, mouth-breathing, drinking water, etc. Sometimes infertility patients are instructed to take oral temperatures to encourage compliance, but many natural family planning counselors recommend rectal or vaginal temperatures. Serena of Canada recommends vaginal temperatures. I personally prefer the vaginal temperature after trying them all.

Dr. Edward Keefe, however, has maintained for decades that the oral temperature is fine for natural family planning. In fact, he states that a woman may quietly get up and go about her morning activities with the thermometer in her mouth. He has conducted small comparative studies with his patients using rectal temperatures plus immobilization, versus quietly moving around for five minutes with a thermometer in their mouths. He found no significant difference in temperature curve or days of abstinence required.[1] I would recommend taking the oral temperature for 8-10 minutes.

Dr. Vollman felt that the rectal temperature was most accurate. Taking the temperature rectally may be uncomfortable for some women, especially if they have hemorrhoids. You may take your temperature at any location you wish, but stay with the same location for the whole cycle. If you use Dr. Vollman's Rule of the mean which compares temperatures from cycle to cycle, do not vary the location at all. If you take your temperature rectally, use a disposable cover or disinfect the thermometer daily. If you use an electronic digital thermometer, always use probe covers and throw them away after use, no matter which oriface you use. If your oral temperature seems to create a curve which is difficult to interpret, try the rectal or vaginal approach for a cycle. Rectal temperatures are not subject to outside influences. Vaginal temperatures are also steady and seem to me to be somehow appropriate.

FACTORS AFFECTING THE WAKING TEMPERATURE

You must be on the lookout for factors affecting the waking temperature. If you are up a lot at night, especially with a sick child,
your temperature can be affected either up or down. Note this
kind of unrestful and stressful night on your chart. If this reading
provided the first high temperature of the cycle, do not count it
as one of the three high temperatures to establish the postovulatory
phase. If it represented the third high temperature and your other
signs such as mucus, etc. confirmed the rise, you can count it.
You can record a low temperature from getting chilled at night;
an electric blanket can give a false high reading. Of course, a high
temperature in the presence of sore throat, fever, or any illness
is not to be counted. If you drink alcohol the night before it can
raise your morning temperature, so don't be fooled. If you drink
the night before and then sleep in, your temperature will jump
off the top of the chart! Sometimes alcohol consumption can even
cause the temperature to be lower. Any temperature compromised
by alcohol must be viewed with skepticism and should not be
counted toward establishing a sustained rise.

EARLY OR LATE WAKING TEMPERATURE

You should try to take your temperature at approximately the same
time each morning and after the same amount of sleep. This isn't
always possible, especially if you have children. You can get a good
reading after about three hours of sleep, and, in a pinch, even
one hour of complete rest will do.[2] If your sleep was disturbed
you should note the circumstances on your chart for consideration in interpreting the chart.

Dr. Joseph Roetzer of Austria, who has counseled natural family
planning for many years, believes that up to one and a half hours
difference between the earliest and latest readings throughout the
cycle makes no significant difference if taken prior to 7:30 AM.[3]

Late temperatures are higher than early temperatures. If you
usually take your temperature at 6:00AM each morning and then

take it at 8:00AM on the weekend, it will affect the biphasic curve. You could either set the alarm for 6:00, take your temperature, and then go back to sleep; or you could adjust the temperature for lateness. Statistical regression analysis of waking temperatures done by Royson and his co-workers[4] produced an adjustment factor of about .1°C per hour to bring temperatures of unusual waking times to a norm. They suggested adjusting the waking temperature for time by adding .1°C for every hour earlier than the norm and subtracting .1°C for every hour later than the norm. Their adjustment factor was actually .086°C, but they rounded it to .1°C for ease of application. Their adjustment factor of .086° Centigrade translates to approximately .15° Fahrenheit per hour (one and a half tenths of a degree per hour). So if you wake up early, you can add .1°F for each 40 minutes. If you sleep in you can subtract .1°F for each 40 minutes. Note the fact of an adjustment on your chart.

FAHRENHEIT OR CENTIGRADE

Most of the people of the world use the metric system of weights and measures and a Centigrade temperature scale. The United States is alone in using ounces, inches, and the Fahrenheit scale. The Fahrenheit scale has smaller units of measure than the Centigrade scale. Freezing is designated as 32° and water boils at 112°. The Centigrade degree (or tenth of a degree) is almost twice the size of the Fahrenheit degree. On the Centigrade scale, freezing is 0° and water boils at 100°.

Centigrade fever thermometers are suitable for natural birth control because each tenth of a degree is shown on the thermometer. A Centigrade tenth of a degree represents a larger unit of heat than a Fahrenheit tenth of a degree. The body must heat up markedly for the temperature to jump to the next single tenth of a degree.

Dr. Vollman much preferred the Centigrade scale. This was not just because he was from Europe, but because he thought that a larger unit of measure was better. You might think that the tiniest, most precise unit of measure would be best, but that may not be the case with natural birth control. We need accuracy but not necessarily subtlety for charting the waking temperature. We need to document a *substantial and unequivocal* rise in temperature rather than small erratic changes. Dr. Vollman felt that it smoothed and simplified the curve to use the Centigrade scale rather than Fahrenheit.

When applying the temperature rule, the basal temperature must rise .2 °C over the six previous lower readings. The World Health Organization Task Force originally defined a significant rise in temperature as .2 ° Centigrade. This was translated to .36 ° Fahrenheit. For natural family planning it is generally rounded up to .4 °F. Two tenths of a degree Centigrade is less of a rise than .4 ° Fahrenheit, and consequently easier to reach; another advantage of the Centigrade scale for natural family planning.

If your chart is choppy and hard to interpret, with temperatures frequently skipping up or down by .1 °F and compromising your count of high temperatures for a sustained rise, you might want to try the Centigrade scale. I have used a Centigrade thermometer for many years and like the ease of interpreting my chart.

Centigrade thermometers are difficult to find. They are sometimes available through hospital supply houses. The one I use came from West Germany and is a large, rather odd looking thermometer meant for axillary (underarm) temperatures. It has served me well.

If you want to try the Centigrade scale and can't obtain a Centigrade thermometer, you can use a Fahrenheit "ovulation" thermometer and convert the temperatures using Table 1. In preparing this table, I carried the conversion to the fourth decimal place. You only need to use the whole number and the first decimal to register your temperature rise in tenths of a degree, but I included the other decimal places because I thought the pattern of numbers was very interesting from a mathematical point of view.

Table 1. CONVERSION OF FAHRENHEIT TO CENTIGRADE

Fahrenheit	=	Centigrade	Fahrenheit	=	Centigrade
97.0		36.1111	98.0		36.6666
97.1		36.1666	98.1		36.7222
97.2		36.2222	98.2		36.7777
97.3		36.2777	98.3		36.8333
97.4		36.3333	98.4		36.8888
97.5		36.3888	98.5		36.9444
97.6		36.4444	98.6		37.0000
97.7		36.4999	98.7		37.0555
98.8		36.5555	98.8		37.1111
97.9		36.6111	98.9		37.1666

CHAPTER 7

NATURAL BIRTH CONTROL AND BREASTFEEDING

Natural regulation of conception is accomplished by interpreting natural symptoms and signs observed during the menstrual cycle. During the period of lactation there may be no ovulation and therefore no cycle. However, it is still possible and often desirable to record the natural signs in anticipation of signs of fertility that hail the approach of the first postpartum ovulation if the parents wish to plan their families the natural way.

This chapter will explain the physiological basis of infertility resulting from a special, *biological,* type of breastfeeding. Concerning effectiveness, I will offer a statistical approach with evidence gathered from clinical experience with varying practices of nursing mothers. It is helpful to have an understanding of the "odds" of becoming pregnant while nursing as well as the natural signs which are sometimes inconclusive at this special time of unusual hormonal influences.

Mothers who breastfeed in our culture most often only *partially* breastfeed. This means that although they nurse their baby, they also give supplemental formula or other liquids, provide a pacifier, introduce semisolids early, and encourage baby to sleep the night through. The baby is then weaned, or partially weaned, at six weeks to three months of age. This has become the most common breastfeeding practice in our modern societies. This regimen offers little if any benefit in fertility regulation.

With *biological breastfeeding,* the baby is nursed on demand throughout the day and night. No supplementary formula, liquids or baby foods are given for about the first six months, and then selected semisolid foods are introduced *gradually* and in *small* amounts. A pacifier is not provided. Biological nursing is known to suppress ovulation, and therefore fertility, for six months to a year or even longer.

Each time the infant nurses, the pituitary gland rapidly secretes a hormone called prolactin. Prolactin suppresses the pituitary hormone FSH and, therefore, ovulation. There is a direct relationship between baby's sucking and the amount of prolactin released. The *frequency* and *duration* of nursing determines the levels of prolactin in the mother's bloodstream. Nursing in the afternoon and at night stimulates more prolactin. So when you start to introduce semisolid foods, give small amounts in the morning. Do not replace an evening feeding with baby food in order to encourage the baby to sleep longer if you want to maintain prolactin levels and enjoy natural infertility at this time.

In a natural setting, where baby is suckled on demand and given no other source of nourishment, the resulting anovulation protects the child from being usurped from the breast by a sibling. This is obviously nature's way of spacing children.

Only the *fully breastfeeding* mother can anticipate infertility of many months duration. Any supplementing of bottle feedings or baby foods will diminish prolactin levels and accelerate the return to ovulation. Biological breastfeeding usually consists of at least six or seven feedings per 24 hour day, each of 10 to 20 minutes duration. When the baby is new, she will usually nurse 7 to 10 times daily for the first few weeks. Then frequency of suckling gradually decreases. Usually, when the baby is about six weeks old, she will begin to sleep longer periods, up to four or five hours, after the evening feeding (9 - 11:00 PM). By four to six months, she may sleep five to seven hours before the early morning feeding.

CLINICAL OBSERVATIONS OF FERTILITY DURING LACTATION

If your baby is nourished by mother's milk exclusively for the first six months, and soft food is introduced gradually during the second six months, your period usually will not return until 9 - 18 months after childbirth, depending on the frequency of suckling and rate of introduction of other foods.[1] Consequently, most women who are *fully* breastfeeding, including night feedings, will remain infertile for about nine months postpartum, and will not observe signs of fertility or resume their menstrual periods. However, about 5% of fully breastfeeding mothers experience a return to fertility between four and six months postpartum. You should begin checking for signs of fertility about four months after the birth.

A study by Howie and McNeilly[2] indicates that when introduction of foods to biologically nursed thriving babies is very gradual, the mother is more likely to have one or two cycles that are not ovulatory. However, with abrupt weaning or sudden reduction in nursing, the first cycle is likely to be fertile.

In a group of otherwise non-contracepting women in Chile, Dr. Soledad Diaz[3] found that half the women ovulated before their first menstrual period and the other half did not. In other words, half had a warning that they were returning to fertility and the other half had an ovulatory, fertile first cycle. He also found that the probability of pregnancy was only 2% for those who had not resumed menstruation and 25% for those who had.

In a study of lactating Australian women[4] only 14% of the women considered to be biologically nursing and 20% of partially lactating women ovulated before the first period compared to 60% of the weaned or weaning group. In this study, there was only a 2% probability of ovulation preceding the first period within the first four and a half months postpartum. Another investigation by Peter W. Howie et al[5] showed that none of the women ovulated while they nursed with no supplements whatsoever. A study by Dr. Adolfo Perez[6] demonstrated that the chances of fully nursing mothers ovulating in the first 10 weeks were practically nil, and from the 11th to the 24th week (6 months) were less than 5%. Based on ultrasound and hormone studies, Dr. Anna Flynn[7] found that in fully breastfeeding mothers, ovulation is often delayed until weaning is begun and usually occurs between 32 and 79 weeks postpartum with an average of 48 weeks. Nursing mothers who supplement early and in increasing amounts usually resume fertility about as quickly as non-breastfeeders[8] in which ovulation occurs within 36 to 77 days postpartum.[9]

Some mothers who return to work early pump and refrigerate their milk to be given while they are away. Often, supplemental food and liquids are also given by the caretaker. In this situation, giving the mother's milk by bottle will benefit baby but *will not stimulate prolactin production* and therefore will not prevent ovulation in the mother.

CHARTING THE SIGNS

It is wise to begin observing and charting your natural signs of fertility about the fourth month postpartum if you are fully breastfeeding. You probably will not observe any fertile signs for a few months, but a small number of women who breastfeed do ovulate between the fourth and sixth month. If you can live with a 5% chance of pregnancy, you can wait until the sixth month to begin recording signs. Even if you are biologically breastfeeding, you will then need to begin your careful observation of cervical mucus, and possibly cervix and basal temperature because this is the time you will be starting to introduce food into your baby's diet. If you have been partially breastfeeding, or have weaned the baby to return to work, you should start checking your signs at about two months postpartum.

Changes in cervical mucus is the first symptom of approaching ovulation. Changes in the cervix appear to be the most reliable indication of ovulation.[7] Do not check your cervix for the first two months after childbirth. The uterus and cervix are still involuting for at least two months. You are not fertile during those first two months unless you do not breastfeed. Most doctors advise abstinence from intercourse during the period of involution. Depending on your nursing practices you can wait two to four months to start charting.

In the early months it is easiest to chart the mucus symptom alone, sometimes backed up with the cervix signs. You may experience dryness at the vulva. If you wish to have intercourse, it would be prudent to first check the cervix. Some women, however, experience cervical mucus of varying description during lactation and this mucus may or may not signal ovulation. Sometimes a watery discharge is the result of low hormone levels leaving the vaginal walls thin and delicate. Some may result from erosion of the cervix after childbirth.[11] Neither of these types of discharge are caused by estrogen secreted by the ovaries. If you have a constant watery discharge, you should see your doctor as you may need to be treated for cervical erosion or another medically treatable condition.

MUCUS RULES

The thin, clear discharge from hormone-deficient vaginal walls or cervical erosion can make interpretation of the mucus sign difficult during the nursing time. I will briefly outline the rules of the mucus method, but it would be wise for you to seek individual counseling or formal classes for help in interpreting your mucus pattern. Natural family planning teachers can be found through your local Catholic diocese or women's clinic. Some Planned Parenthood clinics will make a referral.

If you have four dry days in a row, you are infertile on that fourth dry night. If you observe dry days, it would be helpful to confirm this with a check of the cervix for firmness, mucus at the os, elevation in the pelvis, and the comparable size of the cervical os before having intercourse. If the cervix is low and firm and does not extrude mucus, you can be quite sure you are indeed infertile.

If you have intercourse, you may see some mucus-like discharge the next day, which most likely would be semen. Sometimes you can get up and walk around after intercourse, bear down while sitting on the toilet, and take a bath in order to evacuate the semen that night. If, after trying the above routine, you still have a discharge the next day, you should wait for four more dry days. Do not tell yourself a story that it is only semen. It may be and it may not be. If you have had four dry days and intercourse on the 4th dry night, and, despite your efforts to evacuate semen, you have a discharge the next day, you may be able to confirm continuing infertility with an *unchanging infertile* cervix and avoid waiting four more days. In general, you should have intercourse only every other dry night to avoid semen covering up the mucus sign.

BASAL TEMPERATURE

It is best to chart basal temperature after six months of biological breastfeeding, or earlier if you are (1) giving supplemental bottle feedings, (2) eliminating night feedings, (3) giving a pacifier, (4) adding soft foods, or (6) pumping your milk. The basal temperature will probably not confirm ovulation for several months, but when it does you will be glad you kept track. The basal temperature will also tell you if your first couple of periods were ovulatory and therefore fertile. On the chart, record all waking temperatures, mucus changes, cervix changes (if you check it), altered nursing routine, and illness of mother or baby.

WEANING

Weaning from *biological* breastfeeding is usually a gradual process, taking place over a period of months. If weaning is slow, your milk will stay in good supply and continue to be a major source of nutrients. When weaning takes place at one year of age or older, you may find that your child's natural curiosity of, and interest in, the food that others eat can make this a very smooth transition.

As your child begins to eat more food, sleep the night and

consume less breast milk, you will need to watch your bodily signs carefully for a return to fertility. You may have a number of episodes of fertile cervical mucus without ovulating. You must abstain from intercourse for four days after each of these instances of fertile mucus. Prolactin levels are falling and, in turn, pituitary hormones are beginning to signal the ovaries. This is potentially a very fertile time.

If you wean your child more abruptly, or if she starts cutting back on her own, you will need to abstain from sex for a few weeks while you wait for ovulation. During sudden weaning the hormones are in flux and even careful monitoring may not anticipate a sudden rush of fertility. So, in this instance, unless you have personal counseling from a trained teacher, it is best to wait for that first rise in temperature signaling the first ovulation and a return to cycling.

When your period returns, you will probably experience two or three erratic cycles with long or short cycle length. Be very careful. This is an especially risky time and caution is advised. You have come this far. Restrict intercourse to the high temperature phase of absolute infertility for three cycles and wait for things to settle down.

FORMULA FEEDING

Many women, especially those who work outside the home, decide to give their baby a formula instead of breastfeeding. Some breastfeed briefly and then change abruptly to formula feeding. If you do not breastfeed, your period will usually return in about 6 to 8 weeks. It is best to wait until your first period occurs and until the involutionary changes in the uterus and cervix are complete. Just about the time you may be feeling up to intercourse, ovulation will probably be taking place. It won't be long until you regain your periods and you can again use natural conception regulation. But be careful. The first few cycles postpartum will probably be erratic even if you did not breastfeed.

CONCLUSION

Aside from its importance for "bonding" and tactile contact between mother and child, breastfeeding is the most "natural" method of child spacing. In a simple traditional society, where mother and baby are together day and night and nursing takes place on demand for 18 to 24 months, children are naturally spaced about two years between births. For breastfeeding to be effective as a reliable method of family planning, it is essential that mother and child remain close together continuously so the baby can nurse on demand throughout the day and during the night. It is the frequent sucking on the nipples that causes the production of the hormone prolactin to remain sufficiently high to suppress ovulation. If the baby is given supplemental foods or formula, especially in the evening to encourage him to sleep through the night, this natural period of infertility becomes unreliable.

Partial breastfeeding necessitates great care and patience in interpreting signs of fertility, as it usually delays a return to normal menstrual cycles.

Biological breastfeeding, as described above, is a lot to ask of mothers in our modern society, and impossible unless they are able and willing to give up working outside the home. But it will appeal to, and be appropriate for, some women. Far from considering it a burden, many women who have experienced biological breastfeeding find it hard to give up the joy, closeness and mutually sensual pleasure of nursing.

CHAPTER 8

PREMENOPAUSE AND NATURAL BIRTH CONTROL

Menopause marks the end of ovulation and cyclic menstrual periods in women. It is preceded by about five years of premenopause, a gradual winding down of the reproductive process. Women do not "go through the menopause;" they arrive at it. They "go through" premenopause.

Menopause usually occurs around the age of 50 with premenopause beginning in the upper 40s. The last several years of a woman's menstrual cycles are usually characterized by shorter than usual cycles, then longer and longer cycles evolve until finally the period disappears. These years will present a woman with both the longest and the shortest cycles of her life with the exception of the time of *menarche*, the beginning of menstrual cycling. In the early months of the premenopause, she may experience cycles as short as 18 - 21 days. Later, she may go for three months without a period.

The sixty months preceding menopause present a challenge to natural birth control because of irregularity. However, if a woman has been observing her signs of fertility, especially cervical mucus and changes in the cervix, she will have little trouble interpreting fertile signs even in the face of irregularity. Of course, when menopause finally does arrive, with the cessation of periods, a woman is no longer fertile because she is no longer ovulating. Officially, one must wait for one year after the last period for assurance that menopause has truly arrived. Toward the end of that year, one can be fairly certain that ovulation is a thing of the past, but to be cautious, birth control should not be abandoned for a full year.

As premenopause progresses, a woman will have more and more anovulatory cycles interspersed with ovulatory ones. There will often be long phases of low temperatures. With some of these anovulatory cycles, she will menstruate, usually with a scant period. With others, she will not menstruate and it will appear as a very long cycle. There may be a series of short, light periods or long stretches with no bleeding at all. Some women experience frequent periods with heavy flow, especially if fibroids are involved, which may necessitate a hysterectomy.

When experiencing long cycles, it can be frustrating to watch the temperature stay low for months, never allowing certainty that ovulation has passed and infertility is assured. In retrospect the monophasic cycle was infertile, but the temperature does not confirm it. However, if you continue to take your temperature, you will be able to tell how often you are ovulating and which of the periods represents a fertile cycle. If you ovulate, a period will follow; if you do not ovulate, a period may or may not follow.

The daily temperature can be an educational tool at this time but intimate awareness of one's cervical mucus and the cervix itself can prove invaluable (see Chapter 3). If you have been observing your cervical mucus and cervix for fertile signs, you will know very well when ovulation is approaching. You will especially note a change from the boring and uneventful state of weeks or months, to a state of potential fertility.

During those "fertile as a rabbit" years, I recommend relying primarily on the temperature sign with other signs used for confirmation, because the mucus sign can occasionally be unreliable. However, during the monotonous monophasic plateau of premenopause, these other signs take on major significance when attempting to clarify the intermittent fertile days.

If you are comfortable using barrier methods, you might want to use them now. Your chance of a fertile ovulation in your late forties is low, so a single barrier should suffice to statistically nullify your chance of pregnancy. If you are not willing to use barrier methods, fairly long periods of abstinence may sometimes be necessary. Fewer and fewer of your cycles will be fertile as time goes on. If you are not on supplemental hormones, the occasional periods of fertility should be obvious.

SYMPTOMS OF THE CLIMACTERIC

The last few years of cycling can be symptomatic with hot flashes, vaginal dryness and fragility, aches, tension and insomnia. These endocrine, somatic and psychic changes are known as the *climacteric*. These symptoms can persist until the body adjusts to lower levels of estrogen. Some women are not affected as seriously as others. Thin women tend to fare worse than those with some body fat. If the symptoms are distressing, there are two possible approaches: nutritional therapy and hormone replacement therapy. If you use the former, you can still employ natural family planning. If you choose hormone replacement, you will obscure the natural signs of fertility and will need to find another method of birth control. If you use natural methods for moral reasons, you will certainly want to try the nutritional option before resorting to drugs.

NUTRITIONAL THERAPY

Eating carefully and supplementing with vitamins can help alleviate some of the effects of premenopause. Vitamin E supplements from natural sources seem to help relieve many of the symptoms associated with low estrogen. 400 I.U. per day is a safe dose of this fat-soluble vitamin. The vitamin B complex can help guard against depression and other mental and emotional symptoms. It is best to obtain the B complex, consisting of many different vitamins, from food. The different B vitamins interact with each other and nature provides a good balance in whole grains and vegetables. Calcium supplements can help prevent bone loss especially when taken with vitamin D and a program of weight bearing exercise. Vitamin D is required for proper absorption of calcium. Most low fat milk contains added vitamin D, but low-fat cottage cheese and yogurt generally do not. Even if you consume low fat dairy products, you should also take one to two grams of calcium daily with 400 mg. of vitamin D. Some brands of orange juice are now supplemented with absorbable calcium and vitamin D. Regular exercise such as walking a mile a day will help prevent weight gain that often comes after a decrease in estrogen, will strengthen bones, and will promote a general sense of well-being.

HORMONE REPLACEMENT THERAPY

Many women choose to supplement estrogen to prevent unpleasant effects of the climacteric and to protect against osteoporosis. Osteoporosis is the loss of bone mass in older people, primarily women. Calcium leaves the bones of some women when they do not have a steady supply of estrogen. In the past, estrogen was often prescribed by itself, but that sometimes caused endometrial cancer because it would stimulate the build-up of endometrium, but not provide for its shedding in menstruation. Currently, most physicians prescribe synthetic progesterone (progestin) for part of the month. This combination of hormones results in a light period even after menopause. This may be a slight bother, but it is protective against the possibility of endometrial cancer which exists with estrogen therapy. Women who start estrogen/progestin supplementation in the late premenopause will not know when they reach menopause because they will continue to have light monthly periods. A new regimen is currently being developed[1] in which estrogen and natural progesterone are given simultaneously and continuously, simulating the pregnant state. This new approach may provide the benefits of estrogen replacement therapy without the necessity of a monthly period persisting into menopause.

Although hormone replacement therapy contains the same hormones as birth control pills, the doses are not high enough to suppress ovulation. Consequently, premenopausal women who have not stopped ovulating, no matter how infrequently, who are on hormone replacement therapy must make provisions for birth control. Hormone replacement therapy is not as strong as oral contraceptives, but the estrogen potent enough to cause abundant glassy cervical mucus, while progestin (often taken for the last 12 days of a synthetic cycle) will cause confusing fluctuations in temperature. For this reason, I must advise women who are in the late premenopause and have had to start hormone supplementation for distressing symptoms of the climacteric to choose another form of birth control over the natural methods. Certainly, if you require hormone supplementation during menopause, there is no problem because ovulation and the need for birth control are things of the past.

PREMENOPAUSE AND THE MUCUS METHOD

A number of women who use natural family planning *and do not supplement hormones* during premenopause prefer the mucus method alone at this time when cycles are frequently anovulatory and monophasic. It can be frustrating if the temperature remains low month after month, never assuring infertility. If you have experience with and confidence in your mucus sign, you may choose to use it as a sole indicator of fertility during premenopause. If this is your choice, I would recommend personal counselling in the mucus method from a qualified teacher who is aware of the subtleties of this sign during the transition of premenopause.

CHAPTER 9

PERIODIC ABSTINENCE

In natural birth control, the corollary to observance of the signs of fertility is periodic abstinence. During the fertile times, the couple must abstain from sexual intercourse in order to avoid pregnancy. Abstinence can be difficult. It seems almost unnatural, in conflict with our basic instinctual drives. People want to make love. It is natural and an expression of love, as well as the means to reproduce. But sometimes we must put aside our instinctual drives in favor of reasoned decisions and consideration for the future.

Most men have a sex drive that can be easily aroused at any time. Many women are, through the influence of their female hormones, more interested in sex during the time surrounding ovulation. All of this is quite natural, but will sometimes have to be restrained in the practice of natural birth control. These instincts and the heightened libido in many women during the fertile time are to some degree for the good of the species, the preservation of homo sapiens in what has often been a dangerous environment for procreation and the safe raising of young. These urges, although historically positive for our species, are not necessarily in harmony with our best interests. There will likely be some degree of inner conflict as we restrain ourselves in any way from "what comes naturally," but sometimes in life we must go for the long range good over immediate gratification in order to enjoy the benefits of a rational life plan.

Abstinence means avoiding all genital contact during the fertile time. Sperm can escape upon sexual arousal with or without ejaculation. They can then merge with fertile mucus outside the vagina, propel themselves via mucus into the vagina, and on to their ultimate destination. It is possible to become pregnant through sex-play that does not involve intercourse.

Some complain that abstinence during the fertile time and intercourse confined to the infertile time has women unable to make love when they are most interested, and able when they are not hormonally predisposed (see page 30 - Changes in Libido). A friend of mine has answered that question very nicely, "If nature does not provide, then her husband must."

It takes understanding and commitment to gracefully incorporate periodic abstinence into marriage. It can be difficult at times, but a lot of things in life demand a disciplined, mature approach. Many couples report that it enhances their appreciation of sexual intercourse when their natural cyclic infertility allows. They speak of a little honeymoon monthly. The cooperation and communication necessary for periodic abstinence can be a positive force in marriage. Couples must talk to each other about sex, affection, family goals. If there is a mutual commitment to practicing natural birth control, the abstinence required is a growth process. It is a challenge and is rewarding in its own way.

SIGNS OF FERTILITY AND BARRIER METHODS

I would like to briefly discuss the use of supplemental barrier methods as an alternative to abstinence during the fertile period. Many couples practicing natural family planning object to barrier methods, such as condoms and diaphragms, on moral grounds. Others do not feel this way. Some people choose the natural methods as a way to avoid hormonal intervention or permanent sterilization. For these couples there may be no overriding commitment to the method itself, but rather a rejection of the alternatives. If there is no philosophical or religious consideration, there may not be tolerance for the required abstinence. Some of these couples may be comfortable with barrier methods of birth control and charting the signs of fertility may appeal to them as a way to reduce the need for barrier methods when possible. The opportunity to occasionally have sex without condom or diaphragm can provide the motivation necessary for detailed record keeping and intimate involvement with one's reproductive processes.

WARNING: the days surrounding ovulation are the fertile days of the cycle. If you have unprotected intercourse on the infertile days of the cycle and then use a barrier method on the fertile days as determined by natural signs, you are putting barrier methods to a difficult test. They have a certain rate of success in preventing pregnancy (See chapter 11 - Studies and Statistics), but the statistics derived from their use are based on their use randomly through the cycle when many days are naturally infertile. If you single out the documented fertile days to depend on barriers you concentrate the risk of pregnancy. If you choose to use barrier methods during the fertile time, may I suggest using two methods at once, ie. condom and diaphragm. This will reduce your chance of pregnancy dramatically.

Again, I understand and respect that there are those who have philosophical and moral difficulties with supplemental contraception. I do not, in any way, suggest that they act against their conscience.

68

AIDS

In this day and age, sex before marriage is dangerous, possibly deadly, due to the growing threat of AIDS. Even the use of condoms cannot guarantee "safe sex" from casual encounters, even with people you have known well but who have known others before you. Condoms are not 100% effective for birth control due to incorrect usage and manufacturing defects. Their use may put the odds in your favor, but these odds are not good enough when your life depends on it.

The only safeguard against AIDS is abstinence before marriage and faithfulness within marriage.

CHAPTER 10

HISTORICAL ASPECTS

Throughout most of human history there have been limited means of fertility regulation. The main variables affecting family size were disease, war, famine, and abortion (which has been practiced since ancient times). In the western world, there were religious sanctions against any form of birth control from Protestant and Catholic churches alike, and the early medical profession supported this edict. Any attempt to limit family size was generally considered anti-family and suggested promiscuity. Even abstinence as a means to avoid conception was not officially accepted by the Vatican until 1880.[1] In 1873, the Congress of the United States passed the "Act of Suppression of Trade In and the Circulation of Obscene Literature and Articles of Immoral Use.[2] This legislation combined pornography, abortifacients and contraceptives such as condoms and outlawed their sale and distribution.

Well into the 1900s there were still no acceptable forms of brith control available except abstinence. Abortion was probably the main means to family size regulation, though it was illegal and endangered the lives of many women. *Coitus interruptus* was a common practice, although not acceptable to the Church. Condoms appeared in the mid 1800s, but were considered distasteful objects and were mainly used to protect against venereal disease. There were various kitchen methods such as vinegar douche, half a lemon as a vaginal barrier, etc.[3] These were probably mildly helpful.

69

In the 1800s there were many theories on fertility in women. Most of these postulated that ovulation occurred during menstruation as it does in lower animals when they are in heat. As early as 1847, Pouchet described intermenstrual pain and the midcycle mucus discharge.[4] In 1883 a German gynecologist, Dr. C.F.N. Cappellman, promoted the idea that a "28 day cycle" could be divided in half and the first half was fertile while the second half was sterile, except for a few days before menstruation.[5] These few days were probably difficult to predict, however. His was the first real method of child spacing by periodic abstinence, but it likely sustained a number of pregnancies for women with long cycles who would have been ovulating during the so-called sterile days.

There were two notable papers on basal temperature in the late 1800s. One was by an Englishman named William S. Squire[6] and the other by an American, Mary Putnam Jacobi, one of the first women physicians.[7] They both noticed the biphasic curve of the basal temperature in women, but neither connected this to ovulation or to the potential for fertility regulation.

In 1905 Theodoor Hendrik van de Velde[8] confirmed Mary Putnam Jacobi's findings. He is generally credited with the discovery of the biphasic temperature curve, although he freely admitted that Mary Putnam Jacobi originated the idea. He reported a pregnancy resulting from a single coitus at midcycle, but in his writing he placed more emphasis on his theory that the temperature drop preceding menstruation caused menstruation. Later, in 1926, he clarified that the corpus luteum was responsible for higher temperatures and that the end of corpus luteum activity caused menstruation. He also clearly stated that the temperature shift was related to ovulation.[9]

In 1923 a Japanese gynecologist, Kyusaku Ogino, published a landmark paper describing how ovulation occurred 12 to 16 days *prior* to menstruation regardless of the length of the cycle.[10] He wrote several more papers during the next decade elaborating on his research.[11,12,13,14] In 1929, in Austria, Hermann Knaus documented the same observations.[15] He later insisted that ovulation took place exactly 15 days before menstruation, day 14 of a 28 day cycle.[16] Both Ogino and Knaus designated family planning formulas allowing for abstinence during the assumed lifespan of egg and sperm. Ogino's formula had a better outcome because it required more days of abstinence, allowing for ovulation from the 12th to the 16th day before menstruation, rather than the single 15th day before menstruation.

In the Encyclical of 1930, *Casti Connubii,* periodic abstinence for spacing births was approved by the Catholic Church.[17] In 1932 Dr. Leo Latz authored a popular book called *The Rhythm of Sterility and Fertility in Women*[18] which used the Ogino formula. It was the origin of the term "Rhythm Method."

In addition to calendar calculations, research into basal temperature and other natural signs of ovulation was productive in the 1930s and 1940s. Many investigators studied the relationship of temperature rise to ovulation. Other doctors and physiologists were documenting the fertile characteristics of cervical mucus. In 1932, the same year that Leo Latz' book on rhythm was so well received, Harvey and Crockett[19] postulated a "safe period" deduced from the temperature curve. Seguy and Simonnet associated changes in cervical mucus with ovulation in 1933.[20] A German Catholic priest, Fr. Wilhelm Hillebrand, was independently teaching a temperature method to his local parish in 1934.[21] He was the first to offer a temperature method of natural family planning, and was persecuted by the Nazis for teaching such a concept.[3]

In 1937 Rudolf Vollman, a German obstetrician in Switzerland, began studying the basal temperature curve. Like many others pursuing this subject, he went to the medical literature and found the papers of Mary Putnam Jacobi and T.H. van de Velde, which confirmed his theories. He began teaching a method of natural family planning that used a rhythm formula of "shortest cycle minus 20" for early infertile days and a temperature chart for the later infertile days. He did not publish his observations until 1940.[22] He also asked his patients to note midcycle pain and mucus flow on their temperature charts.

Rubenstein made important contributions with his work correlating temperature with changes in vaginal cells[23] in 1937; and

Palmer and DeVillers, in 1939, officially attributed the rise in basal temperature to the ovarian hormone progesterone.[24]

During these years, much of the research on temperature, such as the papers of T.T. Zuck,[25,26] was to further the treatment of infertile women rather than for the purpose of birth control. However, a significant number of researchers were Catholic physicians and professors such as Jacques Ferin,[27] interested in using temperature to supplement rhythm in determining infertile days in the second (premenstrual) phase of the cycle.

In 1944 Viergiver and Pommerenke studied the relationship of cervical mucus and basal temperature and stated that the maximum amount of clear, egg-white mucus (Spinnbarkeit) occurred right before the temperature shift.[28] During the 1940s and early 50s, the postovulatory rise in temperature was further documented,[29,30,31,32,33] and the "temperature" or "thermal" method of natural family planning began to supplement the rhythm method for establishing the infertile days after ovulation.

In 1948 Dr. Edward Keefe, an American gynecologist, designed the "ovulation thermometer" which displayed the temperature reading in single tenths of a degree instead of the 2/10 measurement of the fever thermometer. This special thermometer also expanded the scale of the mid-range temperatures since the high temperatures of fever were irrelevant to family planning. He taught his temperature method to thousands of Catholic couples through his instruction leaflet than came with the thermometer. He added illustrations of cervical mucus to his instructions in 1953[5], and in so doing was probably the first to teach the subtleties of the mucus sign for family planning.

That same year, Cohen et al, elaborated on Spinnbarkeit as the most fertile property of cervical mucus in the forum of an academic journal.[34] In 1954 G.K. Döring, a German professor of obstetrics and gynecology, published information on the biphasic cycle with formal rules for establishing the high temperature phase for family planning.[35] He had been influenced by one of Vollman's papers on basal temperature published in 1947.[5]

In 1955 a Canadian couple, Rita and Gilles Breault introduced a temperature-based method of family planning in Canada. As recently as the early 1950s Canada still forbade birth control by law, and the local Catholic leadership was unreceptive to any family planning method but rhythm. The Breaults developed their charting methods independently from reading about the biphasic temperature curve in a European journal. Gilles Breault was a technical specialist and charted Rita's temperature on graph paper. His graph paper had long low rectangles instead of squares, and at first Rita could see no curve. But he saw it, plotted the curve on different graph paper, and the Serena organization of Canada was born. At first their family planning information was passed discretely from friend to friend. Eventually the Canadian government approved their program and even helped support their grass-roots teaching network. Serena is, to this day, one of the most highly organized and best taught of all natural family planning programs, and a standard around the world.

In 1962 Carl G. Hartman published his famous *Science and the Safe Period*,[36] a highly scientific review of current literature on reproductive physiology, and a classic in the natural family planning movement. Dr. Edward Keefe made a major contribution in 1962 with his information on the cervix and its signs of fertility.[37] He described changes in texture, position and openness of the cervix during the menstrual cycle. John Marshall published *The Infertile Period: Principles and Practice*[38] in 1963. This was an important text for natural family planning teachers and users. He utilized a temperature formula and the Ogino rule of "shortest cycle minus 18" for early infertile days.

In the early 1960s in France the natural family planning pioneer couple, Drs. Charles and Abeth Rendu of Paris, initiated the CLER (Centre de Liaisan des Equipes de Recherche) with the help of Francois and Michele Guy of Grenoble with the expressed goal of popularizing temperature rhythm in France. The Guys visited the island of Mauritius in 1965-66 to teach temperature rhythm and established the Action Familiale program there.[39] They were very successful in teaching the temperature method to a simple culture and their studies within this program have been important to the documentation of natural family planning.

During the mid-1960s Dr. Josef Roetzer of Austria was teaching a combined method to a large select population as a Catholic marriage advisor. He instructed them in the use of mucus and temperature to establish the second infertile phase, and a simple "first 6 days" of infertility for the early phase. He had excellent results with this method.

Professor Konald Prem, in 1968, suggested that the first day of fertility in the preovulatory phase should be determined by the formula: "shortest cycle minus 19" instead of 18 as advised by Ogino. If there is a major contraindication to pregnancy, the fourth day of the temperature rise should be considered infertile rather than the third.[40]

In the late 1960s and early 70s an Australian couple, Drs. John and Lyn Billings, researched and developed a method of natural family planning based on cervical mucus.[41] Cyclic changes of cervical mucus had been known since the 1930s, but primarily in relation to infertility treatment. They removed this information from the clinical setting and stated most unequivocally that women could best observe and teach the subtleties of this sign of fertility for themselves, and that it was quite adequate on its own for natural family planning worldwide in all cultures. There were some proponents of temperature or combined methods who incorporated the mucus sign, but the Billings insisted that in their method, this sign would stand alone.

In 1967 the World Health Organization of the United Nations held a meeting on the natural methods of family planning and published a monograph called *Fertility Control by Periodic Abstinence.*[42] Noted scientists, mostly from Europe, set standards on such things as what constituted a significant rise in temperature for the temperature methods. Basal temperature and its application on a large scale was the topic at this international forum.

In 1972 the World Health Organization again brought experts together to discuss natural birth control. This time the topic was cervical mucus and fertility. They discussed all aspects of the mucus sign and published a monograph called, *Cervical Mucus in Human Reproduction.*[43]

A tremendous amount of knowledge in physiology, endocrinology, sociology, and sexuality has been gathered over the last century by medical researchers, Catholic physicians and clergy, infertility specialists, and people who teach and use natural methods. The 1970s and 1980s have witnessed the cooperation of the World Health Organization, the Department of Health Education and Welfare, the Agency for International Development, and the major national and international Catholic family planning organizations in pooling information, establishing guidelines, and sponsoring research and effectiveness studies. This open collaboration and the efforts of all involved have brought the natural methods of family planning to their rightful place as benevolent options in the complex and delicate realm of our reproductive powers and responsibilities.

CHAPTER 11

STUDIES AND STATISTICS

Statistics are tricky, difficult to believe, hard to rely on. It is fairly easy to find published statistics to support almost any thesis. Effectiveness statistics on birth control methods can vary greatly from study to study because there are a number of complex factors involved. It is not a clear-cut situation nor one which easily lends itself to scientific study. It is not possible to do a double-blind study on birth control where some have the method and others a placebo. In presenting these birth control effectiveness studies and statistics, I will try to explain some of the circumstances and quirks of the studies, make sense of conflicting testimony, make fair comparisons. It's not easy. Bear with me.

RETROSPECTIVE AND PROSPECTIVE STUDIES

Retrospective Studies glean statistical information from past history. Investigators gather data from records, files and interviews about events that have already taken place in a natural setting. Retrospective studies are not considered as scientific as prospective studies because subjects can be easily lost to follow-up or they can consist of select groups not representative of the general population. *Prospective Studies*, on the other hand, establish their guidelines and study population before the study begins. People know they are being studied. Follow-up is usually complete regarding dropouts, cause of pregnancy, etc.

Prospective studies can be randomized or self-selecting if they compare two or more methods. In the former, subjects are randomly assigned to a method rather than choosing which method they wish to participate in. There are very few randomized studies on birth control because most people do not want this decision made for them. However, it is possible to randomly assign between two very similar methods in the same category as was done by Wade's Cedars-Sinai study which compared two different methods of natural family planning. Randomized studies are considered more scientific because grouping by previous expertise can be eliminated. This study can better predict the rates of success within a larger population. With a self-selecting study, people are assigned to groups according to preference and these groups are compared.

In most prospective studies couples must convey their intentions of planning a pregnancy well in advance of the cycle in which they conceive. Couples who conceive and later explain that they had a sudden change of plans are usually classified as accidental pregnancies. Marshall explains the reason for this protocol as the fact that some of these couples may be rationalizing an event that was in fact unplanned.[1]

Historically, many studies on natural family planning have been retrospective. They consisted of statistics gathered from private clientele of physicians and lay teachers. These subjects were not ordinary people off the street. They were, for the most part, serious, careful practitioners of a method they consciously sought. These studies were relatively small compared to the massive data available for artificial birth control methods through a retrospective look at public and private clinic experience. There were usually a few hundred women at most, often over years of involvement. These studies are important even if the scientific community ranks them behind prospective studies because they demonstrate the potential for success with well taught, highly motivated couples. The major drawback with these studies is that people who have difficulty with the method tend to drop out early and you are left with an above average study population. Prospective studies are a recent phenomena in the documentation of natural family planning. Marshall conducted the first prospective study of these methods in 1966. However, the bulk of these studies were done after 1978.

TYPES OF STATISTICS

METHOD-EFFECTIVENESS, *a.k.a.* theoretical, biological or physiological effectiveness. Method-effectiveness represents pregnancy rates under conditions with perfect usage of the birth control method with no errors or omissions. Usually you get a figure for method-effectiveness by verifying the reasons for unplanned pregnancy. When you exclude errors in use, i.e. illness, risk-taking, etc., you are left with pregnancies that occur despite correct application of the method. When these details are available, the method-effectiveness can illustrate the *potential* of the method, given high motivation and diligent care.

USE-EFFECTIVENESS reflects the rates of success of a birth control method under real life conditions. Besides frailties of the method itself, use statistics reflect unclear motivation, carelessness, errors in application of understanding, omissions in data, and other evidence of human imperfection. This figure will include pregnancies resulting when couples suddenly, with a change of heart or in a moment of great passion, decide to conceive but neglect to give advance notice to the statisticians.

PEARL INDEX

Effectiveness rates in these studies are determined by the Pearl Index. The Pearl Index expresses the number of pregnancies occurring within 100 woman-years (1200 months) of exposure. One hundred woman-years is usually thought of as 100 women for one year. The index figure is written as a whole digit, as in "a Pearl Index of 2" meaning that two out of 100 women became pregnant in that one year. It can also be expressed as a percentage, i.e. 2% per year.

PEARL FORMULA

$$\text{Rate} = \frac{\text{pregnancies}}{\text{cycles}} \times 1200$$

There are some disadvantages to using the Pearl Index. Certain biases are inherent in the methodology. One bias is that the longer the study, the better the results[2] because women gain experience with the correct use of the method, casual samplers of the methods drop out, and women experience lower fertility with age. The more modern life table, derived from the insurance industry's methods of calculating risk, is used in some modern studies. The life table examines only the first year or two to eliminate the better results of long term users. I believe the Pearl Index is quite adequate for our purpose of comparison, and that the success of long term users should be allowed in the figures as well as the failure of new users. It is confusing to compare the life table with the Pearl Index, so we will use the Pearl Index for the sake of uniformity.

ARTIFICIAL BIRTH CONTROL STATISTICS

Table 2 shows use-effectiveness statistics for artificial methods of birth control using the Pearl Index. Large populations were available for study through public and private birth control clinics.

Even with chemical and mechanical methods of birth control, a good outcome is not guaranteed. Birth control is not easy. All methods except the IUD involve human choices and decision making; and the IUD is virtually off the market in the 80s because of potential serious side effects and the lawsuits which follow. Oral contraceptives provide almost 100% protection if one takes them consistently. Their theoretical effectiveness is unsurpassed, but use-effectiveness studies have documented up to a 4% failure rate even for the mighty pill. Most pregnancies which occur despite the use of oral contraceptives are the result of failure to take the pill in

TABLE 2. *Use-effectiveness Statistics for Artificial Birth Control.*

Method	Investigator	Year	Use	Comments
Oral contraceptives (pills)	Royal College[3]	1974	.34	
	Ryder[4]	1973	4.0	
	Tietze[5]	1970	.07	
	Vessey[6]	1982	.16-.32	different estrogen dose
IUD	Ryder[4]	1973	5.0	
	Vessey[6]	1972	1.3-6.8	different IUDs
Condom	Ryder[4]	1973	10.0	
	Vessey[6]	1982	3.6	
Diaphragm + spermicide	Ryder[4]	1973	17.0	
	Vessey[7]	1974	2.4	
	Vessey[6]	1982	1.9	
Spermicides (Foam)	Bernstein[8]	1971	3.98	
	Ryder[4]	1973	22.0	
	Vessey[6]	1982	11.9	

Notes:

Vessey, 1974 - This study on effectiveness of diaphragms involved older, well-instructed women.

Vessey, 1982 - This large multi-method study included 17,000 women from 17 family planning clinics in the UK over a period of nine years. Their statistics for all methods were exceptionally good.

a consistent manner. Some of these pregnancies are from missing a pill or two midcycle and some are from stopping altogether while still under study. Oral contraceptives have a high dropout rate due to a variety of side effects. Fully 45% of women who start taking birth control pills are no longer taking them by the end of the first year.[9] Dissatisfaction with side effects can cause failure to use the method and in the interim between quitting and finding another suitable method, pregnancy can occur.

Barrier methods of birth control such as condoms, diaphragms and spermicides show a wide range of use-effectiveness rates with failures primarily due to improper or sporatic use. Maturity and

82

experience are important to the successful use of the barrier methods of birth control. Each of these methods has its quirks, but can be effective when care is exercised.

Before we begin our discussion of studies and statistics of natural methods of birth control, I would like to point out an interesting fact that may give some perspective on the subject. The Alan Guttmacher Institute reports that, because contraceptives sometimes fail or couples neglect to use them, *more than half the pregnancies that occur among U.S. women each year are unintended.*[10] How about that!

NATURAL BIRTH CONTROL

The following table shows use-effectiveness and method-effectiveness statistics for natural methods of birth control using the Pearl Index. All of the early studies were retrospective, the later ones prospective. Circumstances of these studies were different and you will find explanatory notes right after the table. T = temperature, M = mucus, C = calculations for early days.

TABLE 3. *Effectiveness Statistics for Natural Birth Control*

Investigator	Year	Type	Method	Use	T,M,C
Traissac and Vincent[11]	1963	retro	0.0	13.7	Strict T
Döring[12]	1967	retro	0.0	.8	Strict T
Bartzen[13]	1967	retro	1.5	19.5	T + C
Roetzer[14]	1968	retro		.7	M/T + C
Rendu and Rendu[15]	1969	retro	0.0	3.2	T + C
Marshall[1]	1968	prosp	5.0	19.3	T + C
			1.2	6.6	Strict T
Guy and Guy[16]	1966	retro	1.02	8.03	T
Ball[17]	1976	prosp	2.9	15.5	M
Marshall[18]	1976	prosp		22.0	T + M
Johnson, Roberts, Spencer[19]	1978	prosp	12.8	27.58	M
			1.87	8.6	T + C
			3.65	15.9	T + M
World Health Organization[20]	1978	prosp	2.8	18.9	M
Rice - WHO[21]	1979	prosp	.93	7.16	T + C
Wade et al[22]	1979	prosp	.93	7.16	T + C
			5.67	39.7	M

NOTES ON STUDIES:

Döring[12] - This study had two groups. One used the Strict Temperature method and the other used Döring's own "Early Days" Formula based on a history of temperatures rather than cycle length. The "Strict" method had 8 pregnancies (Pearl of .8). Of these, one had a cold, five were patient errors and two had incomplete records. His combined method used a calculation for early infertile days of: Fertility starts 6 days before the day of the earliest recorded temperature rise. In the 3.1% use failure rate for the combined method, six women conceived on the 2nd day of elevated temperature. Döring states that conception has never occurred on the 3rd day of higher temperatures. He also says that his group of women was not statistically normal. They were older private patients who had two or more children. But he says it "shows the possibility of receiving good results in a relatively intelligent and highly-motivated group of women."

Bartzen[13] - He called his method the "Temperature Rhythm System." This was a retrospective study of 441 private patients in Duluth from 1961-1965. In the first two years of his study, he instructed these women to consider the first 10 days infertile (Rule of 10: 10 days infertile, 10 days fertile, 10 days infertile). In the last three years he changed the "Early Days" Rule to S-19. This explains his rather high failure rate.

Roetzer[14] - Private marriage counselling. These women were highly motivated, disciplined, carefully monitored. He instructed his clients that the first 6 days were infertile unless cycles were short. The postovulatory infertile phase began when 3 temperatures were recorded .1 °C over the previous six. This temperature rise was not counted until mucus had disappeared and the 3rd temperature had to be .2 °C above the previous six.

Marshall 1968[1] - This was the first prospective study of natural methods. The calculation for the preovulatory infertile period was S − 19 = first fertile day. Marshall's main purpose in this study was to extract method (biological) effectiveness data out of his carefully controlled study.

Ball[17] - In this study of the mucus method, eight pregnancies (nearly half) were the result of intercourse on preovulatory days of sticky, cloudy mucus. Based on Ball's impeccable data, Roetzer estimates a Pearl Index of 10 for so-called infertile mucus.[23]

Marshall 1976[18] - In his study of temperature and mucus, Marshall had 1195 cycles recorded resulting in a Pearl Index identical to the number of pregnancies. His overall Pearl Index was a rather high 22. Of these 22 pregnancies, 13 were due to intercourse on "dry days" in the preovulatory phase yielding a Pearl of 13 for the so-called infertile dry days.

Johnson, Roberts and Spencer[19] - This study had some flaws in that the mucus method was apparently not taught consistently throughout the study, but the calculations + temperature group had a good and informative result.

World Health Organization[20] - This WHO study reported that most pregnancies resulted from couples knowingly taking a chance during the fertile period. The five countries studied were Ireland, India, El Salvador, the Philippines and New Zealand.

Rice[21] - This study is known as the five Nation Study or the Fairfield Study. A Rhythm formula, S – 20 = first fertile day, provided the early infertile days. The Serena Canada subgroup had remarkable compliance and produced a method rating of .45 and a use rating of 4.5.

Wade et al.[22] - The Cedars-Sinai study had great difficulty in recruiting as well as with dropout. Participants were randomly assigned to sympto-thermal or Ovulation Method (mucus). Over half of the couples did not complete the study. Almost 40% of the mucus group became pregnant. This study has been accused of having inadequate teaching in the mucus group.[24.25] However, the authors state that the teaching was good, experts were called in to enhance teaching and monitor the progress of the study.[26] Many of the subjects were unmarried, and dissatisfaction with the methods studied ran high.

Rendu and Rendu[15] - Private marriage counselling practice.

Guy and Guy[16] - This study took place in Mauritius, a remote island in the south seas where many of the subjects were illiterate.

Their understanding and cooperation were excellent and they produced an excellent result.

Traissac and Vincent[11] - In this study 35 of 52 unplanned pregnancies occurred as a result of intercourse in the preovulatory phase, against instructions of this "Strict" Temperature Method.[27]

MUCUS AND STATISTICS

Most of the combined methods involving temperature plus calculations or symptoms have significantly lower failure rates than does mucus observation alone. Marshall had two studies, one using calendar calculations with temperature and the other using mucus with temperature. The first had a Pearl Index of 19 and the second, a Pearl Index of 22. He concluded from his studies that the mucus observation was no improvement over rhythm calculations for determining early infertile days.[18] In a randomized study comparing the temperature + symptoms method with mucus as a sole symptom, Wade et al found three times the number of pregnancies in the latter group. They reported an unacceptably high Pearl Index of 39.7 for mucus and a Pearl Index of 13.7 for mucus *plus* temperature. There were no method failures within the combination group and six pregnancies ascribed to the method used in the cervical mucus group.[22]

In view of the evidence, I must recommend that mucus signs of early days infertility (dry days) be overridden when the calendar calculation or inspection of the cervix suggests possible fertility.

EFFECTIVENESS

Most natural birth control pregnancies result from taking a chance. When abstinence is adhered to during the fertile period the natural methods are very effective. Christopher Tietze, the world famous biostatistician, grouped the "Strict" Temperature Method with oral contraceptives and the IUD as those "most effective."[5] Method-related failure for the "Strict" Temperature is almost nonexistent. The worst use-effectiveness rating for the strict form was 13.7 pregnancies per 100 woman-years in Vincent's study,[11] but there were *no method failures*. The best was in Döring's group with .8 use-effectiveness and no method related pregnancies. Even in Marshall's study with separate figures for the strict form, his use rating was 6.6 and method-effectiveness had a Pearl of only 1.2. For couples with strong contraindications to pregnancy, who wish to use a natural method of birth control, the Strict Temperature Method carries an extremely low risk.

Effectiveness of natural family planning depends more on motivation of the couple, the ultimate aim of family size and the age of the mother than on the regularity of the cycle and the signs. Couples who are trying to limit the size of their families to those already present have a much lower "failure" rate with natural methods than those spacing their children. Rice's study found that couples who planned no more children had a failure rate of 4.83% (method failure: .56%); while those postponing or spacing children had a failure rate of 14.83%.[21] In Marshall's 1968 study with an overall unplanned pregnancy rate of 19.3%, the segment of couples who were spacing their children had a 22% failure rate while those whose stated intention was to limit their families had a failure rate of 11%. Marshall also found in that landmark study that for women who had 5+ children, the use rate was the same as the theoretical rate. Obviously, those couples who were spacing children experienced less pressure to follow the rules and observe the restrictions of this participatory form of birth control.

The extremely variable rates of pregnancy in the studies shown in Table 3 exemplify the "human factor" present. We are not dealing with mathematical equations or other clearcut phenomena; but rather with different levels of *motivation, understanding, sexual adjustment; all highly complex factors*. These statistics show the range of possibilities within the structure and rules of various methods. A method can be rated less than optimal in a use-effectiveness study, but if it is practiced carefully by highly motivated couples to whom it is acceptable, the results can be quite good.

In this chapter you have seen some statistics on natural birth control and also for other common forms of birth control. These figures are shown for casual comparison. Do not take them too seriously. Any method of birth control works only as well as you, personally, make it work.

89

REFERENCES

Chapter 1

1. Nofziger M. A co-operative method of natural birth control. Summertown, Tennessee, The Book Publishing Company, 1976. 128 p.
2. World Health Organization. Biology of fertility control by periodic abstinence. Technical Report Series No. 360. Geneva, World Health Organization, 1967. 20 p.

Chapter 2

1. Collins WP. The physiological basis for natural family planning. In: International Seminar on Natural Methods of Family Planning. (Organized by the Department of Health, Dublin, Ireland, in collaboration with the World Health Organization). Dublin, Ireland, October 8-9, 1979. p.24-41.
2. Speroff L, Vande Wiele RL. Regulation of the human menstrual cycle. Am J Obstet Gynecol 109:234-247,1971.
3. France JT. Biology of the fertile period. Int J Fertil 26:143-152,1981.
4. Moghissi KS, Syner, FN, Evans TN. A composite picture of the menstrual cycle. Am J Obstet Gynecol 114:405-418,1972.
5. Yussman MA, Taymor MI, Miyata J, Pheteplace C. Serum levels of hormone and plasma progestins correlated with human ovulation. Fertil Steril 21:119-125,1970.
6. Moghissi KS. Prediction and detection of ovulation. Fertil Steril 34:89-98,1980.
7. Brown JB. Timing of ovulation. Med J Aust 2 (23):780-783,1977.
8. Cohen MR. Detection of ovulation by means of cervical mucus and basal body temperature. In: Greenblatt RB (ed). Ovulation - Stimulation, suppression and detection. Philadelphia, JB Lippincott, 1966. p. 291-298.
9. Moghissi KS. Sperm migration through the human cervix. In: Elstein M, Moghissi KS, Borth R (eds). Cervical mucus in human reproduction. Copenhagen, Scriptor, 1973. p. 128-149.
10. Hafez ESE, Thibault CG. International symposium on the biology of spermatozoa: transport, survival and fertilizing ability. Fertil Steril 25:825-834,1974.
11. France JT, Boyer KG. The detection of ovulation in humans and its application in contraception. J Reprod Fert (Suppl) 22:107-120,1975.
12. Hafez ESE. Transport and survival of spermatozoa in the female reproductive tract. In: Hafez ESE. Human semen and fertility regulation in men. St. Louis, CV Mosby Company, 1976. p. 107-129.
13. Vander Vliet WL, Hafez ESE. Survival and aging of spermatozoa: a review. Am J Obstet Gynecol 118:1006-1015,1974.
14. Odeblad E. Micro NMR in high permanent magnetic fields. Acta Obstet Gynecol Scand 45 (Suppl 2):1-188,1966. p.127.
15. Hafez ESE. Histology and microstructure of the cervical epithelial secretory system. In: Elstein M, Moghissi KS, Borth R. Cervical mucus in human reproduction. Copenhagen, Scriptor, 1973. p.23-32.
16. Pommerenke WT. Cyclic changes in physical and chemical properties of cervical mucus. Am J Obstet Gynecol 52:1023-1031,1946.
17. Fordney-Settlage D. A review of cervical mucus and sperm interactions in humans. Int J Fertil 26 (3):161-169,1981.
18. Moghissi KS. The function of the cervix in fertility. Fertil Steril 23:295-305,1972.

90

19. Hilgers TW, Abraham GE, Cavanaugh D. Natural family planning. I. The peak symptom and estimated time of ovulation. Obstet Gynecol 52:575,1978.
20. Cohen MR. Methods of determination of ovulation. J Reprod Med 1:181-186,1968.
21. Hanson FW, Overstreet JW. The interaction of human spermatozoa with cervical mucus in vivo. Am J Obstet Gynecol 140:173-177,1981.
22. Insler V, Glezerman M, Zeidel L, Bernstein D, Misgav N. Sperm storage in the human cervix: a quantitative study. Fertil Steril 33:288-296,1980.
23. Clos JA. De l'influence de la sund sur la menstruation. Bull Acad Roy Sci (Belgique), 2e série, 4:108-160,1858. As cited in: Vollman RF. The menstrual cycle. Philadelphia, WB Saunders Company, 1977. p 1-2.
24. Hume K. Recent advances in the ovulation method. Aust Fam Physician 3:150-157,1974.

Chapter 3

1. Lanctot CA. Natural family planning. Clin Obstet Gynecol 6:109,1979.
2. Parenteau-Carreau S. Love and life. Ottawa, Serena Canada, 1975.
3. Brennan JJ, Klaus H. Terminology and core curricula in natural family planning. Fertil Steril 38:117-118,1982.
4. France JT. Biology of the fertile period. Int J Fertil 26:143-152,1981.
5. Flynn AM. Cervical mucus and identification of the fertile phase of the menstrual cycle. Br J Obstet Gynecol 83:656-659,1976.
6. Billings EL, Billings JJ, Catarinich M. Atlas of the ovulation method, ed. 4. Melbourne, Advocate Press, 1980.
7. Keefe EF. Self-observation of the cervix to distinguish days of possible fertility. Bull Sloane Hospital for Women 8:129-136,1962.
8. Keefe EF. Cephalad shift of the cervix uteri: sign of the fertile time in women. Int Rev Nat Fam Plann 1:55-60, 1977.
9. Iannone B, Iannone F, Parenteau-Carreau S. The cervical palpation (pamphlet). Ottawa, Serena Canada, 1979.
10. Flynn AM, Lynch SS, Docker M, Morris R. Clinical, hormonal and ultrasound indicators of returning fertility after childbirth. In: Proceedings of the XIth World Congress on Fertility and Sterility, Dublin, June 1983. pp. 325-335.
11. Vollman, RF. The premenstrual phase of the menstrual cycle. Int Rev Nat Fam Plann 1:322-330,1977.
12. O'Herlihy C, Robinson HP. Mittelschmerz is a preovulatory symptom. Br Med J 280:286,1980.
13. Hartman CG. Science and the safe period. Baltimore, Williams & Wilkins Company, 1962.
14. Watson PE, Robinson MF. Variations in body weight of young women during the menstrual cycle. Br J Nutr 19:237-248,1965.
15. Englander-Golden P, Chang HS, Whitmore MR, Dienstbier RA. Female sexual arousal and the menstrual cycle. J Human Stress 6:42-48,1980.
16. Moss RH, Kopell BS, Melges FT, et al. Fluctuations in symptoms and moods during the menstrual cycle. J Psychosom Res 13:37-44, 1969.
17. Adams DB, Gold AR, Burt AD. Rise in female-initiated sexual activity at ovulation and its suppression by oral contraceptives. N Engl J Med 299:1145-1150,1978.
18. Udry JR, Morris NM. Distribution of coitus in the menstrual cycle. Nature 220:593-596,1968.
19. Persky H, O'Brien CP, Khan MA. Reproductive hormone levels, sexual activity and moods during the menstrual cycle. Psychosom Med 38:62-63,1976.

20. Gray DS, Gorzalka BB. Adrenal steroid interactions in female sexual behaviour: a review. Psychoneuroendocrinology 5:157-175,1980.
21. Speroff L. Hormonal events and disorders of the menstrual cycle. In: Gynecologic endocrinology. Chicago, Year Book Medical Publishers, Inc.,1977.
22. Bancroft J. Hormones and human sexual behaviour. Br Med Bull 37:153-158,1981.

Chapter 4

1. World Health Organization. Biology of fertility control by periodic abstinence. Technical Report Series No. 360. Geneva, World Health Organization, 1967. 20 p.
2. Kavanagh-Jazrawy F, Pharand-Lapointe M. Planning your family the ST way. Ottawa, Serena Canada, 1975.
3. Marshall J. The infertile period: principles and practice. Baltimore, Helicon Press, 1963. 118 p.
4. Lanctot CA. Natural family planning. Clin Obstet Gynecol 6:109-127,1979.
5. France JT. Biology of the fertile period. Int J Fertil 26:143-152,1981.

Chapter 5

1. Hartman CG, Cited in: Vollman RF. The menstrual cycle. Philadelphia, WB Saunders Company, 1977.
2. Vollman RF. The menstrual cycle. Philadelphia, WB Saunders Company, 1977.

Chapter 6

1. Keefe EF. Physicians help make rhythm work. NY State J Med 76:205-208,1976.
2. Parenteau-Carreau S. Love and life (brochure). Ottawa, Serena Canada, 1975.
3. Roetzer J. Supplemented BBT and regulation of conception. Int Rev Nat Fam Plann 4:1-18,1980. Translation by Huneger RJ of: Rotzer J. Erweiterte Basaltemperaturmessung und Empfängnisregelung. Arch Gynaekol 206:195-214,1968.
4. Royston JP, Abrams RM, Higgins MP, Flynn AM. The adjustment of basal body temperature measurements to allow for time of waking. Br J Obstet Gynecol 87:1123-1127,1980.

Chapter 7

1. Jackson RL. (1987) Personal communication.
2. Howie PW, McNeilly HS. Effect of breastfeeding patterns on human birth intervals. J Reprod Fertil 65:545-557,1982.
3. Diaz S. Breastfeeding and the return of menses, ovulation and fertility. Int J Fertil (in press).
4. Gross BA. Breastfeeding and natural family planning. Int J Fertil (in press).
5. Howie PW, McNeilly AS, Houston MJ, et al. Fertlity after childbirth: infant feeding patterns, basal PRL in levels and postpartum ovulation. Clin Endocrinol 17:315-322,1982.
6. Perez A. Natural family planning: postpartum period. Int J Fertil 26:219-221,1981.
7. Flynn AM, Lynch SS, Docker M, Morris R. Clinical, hormonal and ultrasonic indicators of returning fertility after childbirth. In: Proceedings of the XIth World Congress on Fertility and Sterility, Dublin, June 1983. Lancaster, UK, MTP Press,

1984. pp. 325-335.

8. Tietze C. The effect of breastfeeding on the rate of conception. In: Proceedings of the International Conference, New York, 1961 Vol. II. London, London International Union for the Scientific Study of Population,1961. p. 129-136.

9. Perez A, Vela P, Masnick GS, Potter RG. first ovulation after childbirth - the effect of breastfeeding. Am J Obstet Gynecol 114:1041-1047,1972.

10. Flynn AM. A survey of postpartum fertility studies with particular reference to the breastfeeding mother. Int J Fertil 26:203-208,1981.

11. Taylor RS. Physiology of the vagina and cervix in breastfeeding women. In: Shivanandan M (ed.). Breastfeeding and natural family planning: selected papers from the Fourth National and International symposium on Natural Family Planning. Bethesda, K.M. Associates, 1986.

12. Collins WP. The physiological basis for natural family planning. p. 24-41 In: International Seminar on Natural methods of Family Planning. (Organized by the Department of Health, Dublin, Ireland in collaboration with the World Health Organization). Dublin, Ireland, October 8-9, 1979.

13. Hatherley LI. Late infertile days in early postpartum cycles. Clin Reprod Fertil 3:73-80,1985.

Chapter 8

1. Hargrove, J. (1987) Personal communication.

Chapter 10

1. Potts M, Diggory P. Textbook of contraceptive practice. 2nd ed. Cambridge, Cambridge University Press, 1984.

2. Ibid.

3. Vollman RF. (1979) Personal communication.

4. Pouchet FA. Théorie positive de l'ovulation spontanée et de la fécondation des mammifères et de l'espèce humaine, basée sur l'observation de toute la série animale. Paris, Baillière, 1847.

5. Mucharski J. History of the biologic control of human fertility. Oak Ridge, NJ, Married Life Information, 1982.

6. Squire W. Puerperal temperatures: transactions of the Obstetrical Society, London, 9:129,1868.

7. Vollman, RF. The menstrual cycle. Philadelphia, WB Saunders Company, 1977.

8. van de Velde TH. Ueber den Zusammenhang zwischen Ovarialfunktion, Wellenbewegung, und Menstrualblutung, und ueber die Entstehung des sogenannten Mittelschmerzes. Haarlem, Bohn, 1905.

9. van de Velde TH. Die Vollkommene Ehe: Eine Studie ueber ihre Physiologie und Technik. Leipzig, Stuttgart, Benno Konegan, 1926.

10. Ogino K. Researches on human corpora lutea. Hokuetsu Med J 38:1,1923.

11. Ogino K. Period of ovulation, relation between corpora lutea and cyclical changes in the uterine endometrium; cyclical changes in the uterine endometrium and fertile time. Jpn Gynecol J 19,1924.

12. Ogino K. Histological studies on corpora lutea, period of ovulation, relation between corpora lutea and cyclic changes in uterine mucus membrane, and the period of fertlization. Jpn Med World 8:147,1928.

13. Ogino K. Ovulationstermin und Konzeptionstermin. Zentralbl Gynaekol 54:464-479,1930.

14. Ogino K. Ueber den Konzeptionstermin des Weibes und seine Anwendung in der Praxis. Zentralbl Gynaekol 57:721,1932.

15. Knaus H. Die periodische Frucht- und Unfruchtbarkeit des Weibes. (Periodic fertility and infertility in women.) Zentralbl Gynaekol 56:1393-1408,1933.

16. Knaus H. Ueber die Berechnung des Geburtenregelung. Die periodische Fruchtbarkeit und Unfruchtbarkeit des Weibes. Zentralbl Gynaekol 63:194,1939.

17. Potts M, Diggory P. Textbook of contraceptive practice. 2nd ed. Cambridge, Cambridge University Press, 1984.

18. Latz L. The rhythm of sterility and fertility in women. Chicago, Latz Foundation, 1932.

19. Harvey OL, Crockett HE. Individual differences in temperature changes of women during the course of the menstrual cycle. Hum Biol 4:453-468,1932.

20. Seguy J, Simonnet J. Recherche de signes directs d'ovulation chez la femme. Gynéc Obstét 28:657-663,1933.

21. Vollman RF. The menstrual cycle. Philadelphia, WB Saunders, 1977.

22. Vollman RF. Variationsstatistiche Analyse der Phasen des Genitalzyklus der Frau durch Auswertung des Intermenstrualschmerzes als Indikator fuer den Ovulationstermin. Mschr Geburtsh Gyn 110:115-137,1940.

23. Rubenstein BB. the relation of cyclic changes in human vaginal smears to body temperature and basal metabolic rates. Am J Physiol 119:635-641,1937.

24. Palmer R, Devillers J. Thermal action of sexual hormones in women. C Rend Soc Biol 130:895-896,1939.

25. Zuck TT. The relation of basal body temperature to fertility and sterility in women. Am J Obstet Gynecol 36:998-1005,1938.

26. Zuck TT. The time of fertility and sterility during the human menstrual cycle. Ohio State Med J 35:1200-1203,1939.

27. Ferin J. Détermination de la période sterile prémenstruelle par la courbe thermique. Brux Méd 27;2786-2793,1947.

28. Viergiver E, Pommerenke WT. Meansurement of the cyclic variations in the quantity of cervical mucus and its correlation with basal temperature. Am J Obstet Gynecol 48:321-328,1944.

29. Halbrecht I. Ovarian function and body temperature. Lancet 2:668-669,1945.

30. Barton M, Wiesner BP. Waking temperature in relation to female fecundity. Lancet 2:663-668,1945.

31. Martin PL. Detection of ovulation by basal temperature curve with correlating endometrial studies. Am J Obstet Gynecol 46:53-62,1943.

32. Palmer A. A diagnostic use of basal temperature in gynecology and obstetrics. Obstet Gynecol Surv 4:1-26,1949.

33. Israel SL, Schneller O. The thermogenic property of progesterone. Fertil Steril 1:53-65,1950.

34. Cohen MR, Stein IF, Sr., Kaye BM. Spinnbarkeit: a characteristic of cervical mucus; significance at ovulation time. Fertil Steril 3:201-209,1952.

35. Döring GK. Die Bestimmung der fruchtbaren und unfruchtbaren Tage der Frau mit Hilfe der Koerpertemperatur. Stuttgart, Thieme Verlag, 1954.

36. Hartman CG. Science and the Safe Period. Baltimore, Williams and Wilkins Company, 1962.

37. Keefe EF. Self-observation of the cervix to distinguish days of possible fertility. Bull Sloane Hosp for Women 8(4):129-136,1962.

38. Marshall J. The infertile period: principles and practice. Baltimore, Helicon Press, 1963. 118 p.

39. Guy F, Guy M. Ile Maurice: regulation des naissances et action familiale. Lyon, Editions Xavier Mappus,1968.

40. Prem KA. Temperature method in the practice of rhythm. Child Fam 7:311,1968.

94

41. Billings JJ. The ovulation method. Melbourne, Australia, Advocate Press, 1970. 96 p.
42. World Health Organization. Biology of fertility control by periodic abstinence (Tech Rep Ser 360). Geneva, World Health Organization,1967.
43. World Health Organization. Cervical mucus in human reproduction. Copenhagen, Scriptor,1973.

Chapter 11

1. Marshall J. A field trial of the basal-body-temperature method of regulating births. Lancet 2:8-10,1968.
2. Potter RG. Length of the observation period as a factor affecting the contraceptive failure rate. Milbank Mem Fund Q 38:140-152,1960.
3. Royal College of General Practitioners. Oral contraceptives and health: an interim report. London, Pitman, 1974.
4. Ryder NB. Contraceptive failure in the United States. Fam Plann Perspect 5:133-152,1973.
5. Tietze C. Relative effectiveness. In: Calderone MS. Manual of family planning and contraceptive practice. 2nd ed. Baltimore, Williams and Wilkins Company,1970. pp 268-275.
6. Vessey M, Lawless M, Yeates D. Efficacy of different contraceptive methods. Lancet 1:841-842,1982.
7. Vessey MP, Wiggins P. Use-effectiveness of the diaphragm in a selected family planning clinic population in the United Kingdom. Contraception 9:15-22,1974.
8. Bernstein GS. Clinical effectiveness of an aerosol contraceptive foam. Contraception 3:37-42,1971.
9. Greep RO, Koblinsky MA, Jaffe FS. Reproduction and human welfare: A review of the reproductive sciences and contraceptive development. Cambridge, MIT Press, 1976,p.64.
10. Ory HW, Forrest JD, Lincoln R. Making choices-evaluating the health risks and benefits of birth control methods. New York, The Alan Guttmacher Inst., 1983.
11. Traissac R, Vincent B, Vincent A. Continence périodique et Méthode des témperatures. La Revue de médecine janvier, 1963:11.
12. Döring GK. Reliability of temperature records as a method of contraception. In: Greenhill JP, ed. The year book of obstetrics and gynecology, 1968. Chicago, Year Book Medical Publishers, Inc., 1968.
13. Bartzen PJ. Effectiveness of the temperature rhythm system of contraception. Fertil Steril 18:694-706,1967.
14. Roetzer J. Supplemented BBT and regulation of conception. Int Rev Nat Fam Plann 4:1-18,1980. Translation by R.J. Huneger of: Rötzer J: Erweiterte Basaltemperaturmessung und Empfängnisregelung. Arch Gynaekol 206:195-214,1968.
15. Rendu C, Rendu E. Premiers résultats de l'enquéte sondage du CLER. fiches documentaires du CLER 37:71,1966.
16. Guy F, Guy M. Ile Maurice - résultats d'un sondage. fiches Documentaires du CLER 34:19,1966.
17. Ball M. A prospective field trial of the "Ovulation Method" of avoiding conception. Eur J Obstet Gynecol Reprod Biol 6:63-66,1976.
18. Marshall J. Cervical-mucus and basal-body-temperature method of regulating births: field trial. Lancet 2:282-283,1976.
19. Johnson JA, Roberts DB, Spencer RB. A survey evaluation of the efficacy and efficiency of natural family planning services and methods in Australia. Report of a research project. Sydney, St. Vincent's Hospital,1978. 436. pp.

20. World Health Organization, Task Force on Methods for the Determination of the Fertile Period, Special Program of Research, Development, and Research Training in Human Reproduction. A prospective multicenter trial of the ovulation method of natural family planning. II: The effectiveness phase. Fertil Steril 36:591-598,1981.

21. Rice FJ, Lanctot CA, Garcia-Devesa C: Effectiveness of the sympto-thermal method of natural family planning: an international study. Int J Fertil 26:222-230,1981.

22. Wade ME, McCarthy P, Braunstein GD, Abernathy JR, Suchindran CM, Harris GS, Danzer HC, Uricchio WA: A randomized prospective study of two methods of natural family planning. Am J Obstet Gynecol 141:368-376,1981.

23. Roetzer J: fine points of the sympto-thermic method of natural family planning. No. 2. Tokyo, Japan, Japan Human Life Foundation, 1977. 36 p.

24. Billings JJ: Two methods of natural family planning (letter). Am J Obstet Gynecol 136:697-698,1980.

25. Hilgers TW: Two methods of natural family planning (letter). Am J Obstet Gynecol 136:696-697,1980.

26. Wade ME, McCarthy P, Harris GS, Danzer HC. Reply to Dr. Hilgers (letter). Am J Obstet Gynecol 136:697,1980.

27. Lanctot CA, Parenteau-Carreau S. Studies of the effectiveness of temperature methods of family planning. In: Uricchio WA, ed. Proceedings of a research conference on natural family planning. Washington, DC. The Human Life Foundation, 1973. pp. 311-316.

Index

The publisher and the author do not guarantee the methods of birth control described in these pages. No method of birth control is 100% effective, not even sterilization. The effectiveness of natural birth control is highly dependent on the care taken in application of the method. And, as with all methods of birth control, there is a small chance of failure of the method itself.

You may order this book from the publisher:
MND Publishing, Inc.
P.O. Box 210813
Nashville, TN 37221

For each copy, send check or money order for $6.95 (postage included). TN residents please add $.54 sales tax.

Temperature charts are available: 12 8½"×11" sheets for $3.00 (postage included). TN residents please add $.23 sales tax.